GOD

AS

MOTHER

A True Story of the Search for
Mystic Christianity and Origins of the Soul

GOD
AS
MOTHER

A True Story of the Search for
Mystic Christianity and Origins of the Soul

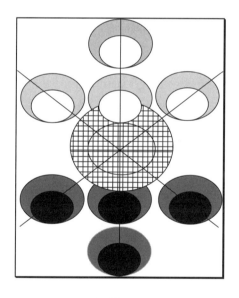

By
Victoria Jennings

InnerSearch Books

FIRST EDITION Published 2002
By InnerSearch Books

Library of Congress Cataloging-in-Publication Data has been
applied for

ISBN# 0-9715748-1-2

Man must diligently seek an understanding of God
Lest he stay in ignorance
and servitude to agencies less divine.

CONTENTS

Acknowledgements

For an introduction into the secrets of all ages, I must thank my first teacher, Catherine Reynolds, who helped prepare my physical vehicle and condition my mind for a life assignment that would come some twenty years later. She was a great teacher who, with patience and understanding, walked me through my first initiations into the mysteries of life.

I had to wait another 20 years for my next significant teacher, Marie Bauer Hall, wife of the late philosopher Manly P. Hall. It was she who carried my life assignment. The first time I heard Marie speak, I knew she was a true channel carrying a message for all mankind. In the words of Manly P. Hall, "She was the most dedicated person I'd ever known." Sixty years of continuous writing by day and night, denying herself and her family – all for the cause of world and family enlightenment. She had understood the true importance of being in service to mankind. She lifted my heart and Soul so that I could travel to a period before time had begun, inspiring me with her visions which had taken her fifty years to see – a cosmogony that brings mystic Christianity, mythology, and science into our age of Enlightenment. Within her works I discovered a pattern, a geometric, mathematical order that lies at the core of all true teachings. This is only my interpretation of Marie's cosmogony and I am in hopes it will encourage others to seek the gems of wisdom still buried within her works.

Next, I am especially grateful to Fred and Ruth Cole. It is through their generosity and support that the funding for this publication was provided. It was Fred who had stood by Marie for fifty years. Believing in and supporting her work, making copies of her transcripts available to the Vatican as well as almost every major government institution in the world. Fred had arranged for the original publication of Marie's works and gave his life to the support of a cause whose time had not yet come. As he fulfilled the duties of *his* life's assignment, he became the "watchman," the record-keeper for lost souls. It was Fred who kept the light burning so that I could access the works as a whole. I thank you, Fred, for sharing what information you had gathered through the years of working with Marie. And I truly appreciate your support and courage in believing that my work was not done in vain.

A special thanks goes to Eleanor Detiger, who had originally been the catalyst through which I had met Marie. Unknowingly you had been placed within the Divine Plan, to set my life's assignment into motion. For this, I will always be grateful.

My sincerest gratitude goes to my family. To my daughters Lisa and Michelle, thank you for your years of patience and understanding toward my work, and thank you for giving me the opportunity to share with both of you the things I have come to understand. To my husband Charles goes my deepest gratitude, for I could not have done it without your encouragement and constant supervision over the simplifying of the material. Thank you for believing in me and for your help in keeping me focused on the true nature of my job in this lifetime and not allowing me to give up. Thank you for accepting me as I am…yet allowing me the space to find what I was to become. You are truly a Soulmate, and I would be honored to join you in the lifetimes to come. And to my Mother Joyce Jennings, thank you. You taught me one of the greatest lessons of them all, that there is nothing too great to be accomplished – it has been engraved within my Soul. And to my brother, Marc, I thank you for helping me with my garden, a place of solace when I stepped away from my computer and was in need of peace.

I would also like to thank my friends, Elnathon Batoon, Trish Planck, Rick Duim (Webmaster), George Navarro, Richard and Helen Sanchez, Phil Mendes, Elise Heafner, Kelly Nine and Vicky Pulatian who took part in our study groups and took the time to help us in organizing the works – you have always been a source of inspiration. Many thanks to all who stood by me, even in times of great darkness who helped me to recognize that my work was not done in vain. Your shining faces lit the pathway to the Great Brotherhood, proving that "Love's Labor's" was not lost.

A special note to my editor, Jasmine Kazarian: she is a true alchemist, for without her enthusiasm, editorial skills, and sensitivity towards a deeper understanding of life, this book could not have been published in its present form. You have been a great comfort and inspiration for me, I am grateful for our friendship.

To The Reader:

God As Mother has an appendix
with additional illustrations and photographs
online.   This supplementary matter is signified
within the book by a keyword in **bold**, followed
by the attachment symbol:
"📎"
Please see our website:
<u>www.godasmother.org</u> and select
"Attachments" for a list of keywords with
added information.

August 26, 1938

Part I

Search For Bruton Vault
Williamsburg, Virginia

In the heavy morning mist just before the light of dawn, three shadowy figures scurried across a pathway and slipped quickly into the cold empty graveyard of Bruton Parish.

As the three entered, the giant tombstones looked like ghosts encircling them, demanding to know, "Why...Why are you here you intruders, infringing upon our sanctuary?!" But there was mystery in the air and by this they were intrigued. So the giant ghosts watched in silence letting the intruders move on.

One figure moved more swiftly and more determined than the rest. Her small, slender body glided easily across the grass, leading the way through the dense blanket of darkness as if she had done this a thousand times before. A second figure, a burly man, struggled to keep up as he carried the heavy shovels and bags of equipment upon his aching back.

The third figure, over-laden by his own bags and shovel, lagged behind, peering into the darkness, keeping a watchful eye. They had to stay low to avoid being seen. They were drawn to a large pyramidal tomb, a monument to David Bray, its dark form barely visible in the gloom.

There, the three figures silently dropped their heavy sacks to the ground. The sun would break soon; time was of the essence. The woman lit a small candle – then unrolled three soft wrinkled sheets of tissue paper upon the ground. It revealed the rubbings she had made from a tombstone nearby. "Here Lyeth Ann Graham," it read. She quickly calculated the dates of birth and

1

death of the deceased and anagrammatically[1] decoded the tracings from the tombstone – forming new sentences and numerical codes.

After adding the numbers, she moved away from the pyramidal tomb and stepped softly across several graves, counting each step along the way. Finally, she stopped. The large burly man quickly pulled a long iron rod from his sack. Following her direction, he raised the rod above his head and thrust it down into the fresh, soft earth piercing deep into its crust...sending off a loud, heavy thud. At a depth of three feet the rod struck something.

Then, just as the first light broke through the mist, the second man joined the first, raising his rod and thrusting it into the earth – again the loud and heavy thud. Now the three quickly grabbed their shovels and started to dig along the line between the two rods. The sound of their shovels scraping the earth and the smell of sweat began to permeate the air. Tiny particles of earth floated gently upward enshrouding the frantic diggers in a luminescent cloud of dust. The sun's rays shown brightly – its light, like daggers, pierced the sky just as the diggers pierce the earth below them. They dug faster...the church vestry and the representatives for the Rockefellers would soon be here.

Suddenly, one of the shovels hit something. The three dug furiously until they made a ditch around the solid form, then stopped. The young woman bent down and gently brushed the final dust away. She knew that these were not rocks or the bricks of an old grave, but the lost foundation of the first and original Bruton Church. Stunned, with tears in her eyes, she whispered, "They said it didn't exist!"

Everyone, even the best historians, had denied its existence. But she had found the foundations by decoding ciphers left on the old tombstones and assembling anagrams she had discovered in rare books left within the musty archives of the

---

[1] Anagram: word or phrase formed from another by transposing the letters.

California museum – where she worked as a translator for rare Alchemical, German Texts.

The surface of the brick was glazed with age and glimmered in radiant colors of light. She wondered how long they were left to lie covered within the earth...and why fate had brought them to see the light again? Many had searched for the old foundation; all had heard the story told a hundred years before of a vault hidden beneath these very bricks; its mysterious contents known only to a select few.

The diggers tore at the earth relentlessly. While their minds were filled with expectation, they feared that someone would come to stop them.

Several hours into the new day, the diggers were near exhaustion but they continued exposing each side of the foundation until it was complete. Finally, with the foundations uncovered, they dropped their shovels to the ground, and then rested their weary bones in the ditches they had dug.

Suddenly an angry voice penetrated the silence, "Stop!"

The old caretaker of the cemetery was running toward them, almost tripping over the graves.

The burly man froze, but the woman only smiled, "It's alright, they can't hide it from us now."

The caretaker began to see the extent of the dig, "What have you done?! You were warned not to interfere!"

But it was too late – the three had found what they had searched for, and the existence of the foundations could no longer be denied!

As she sat there within the ditch, looking up into the sun, the angry voice of the caretaker and everything else melted away. She was at peace. Fate had been her guide and her journey had begun. Something inside her had been transformed; the young woman had now become part of a Divine plan...and from this moment forward her destiny would be the unveiling of its mysteries.

And so the visions began – and she would record, decipher, and diagram all that she would witness for the rest of her long eventful life. Her name was Marie Bauer Hall and her writings – the thousands of typed, and handwritten pages – would become her solace, for only upon those pages could her visions be given reality.

❖

Sixty years after that strange Virginia morning,
a visitor would discover Marie's life's works –
the manuscript pages deteriorating within boxes
and files. The visitor's name, was Victoria...
and fate would be her guide now...

Victoria

Alexandria Bookstore
Pasadena, California

Boom! A loud and heavy thump rang through the store as the UPS deliveryman carted in the heavy boxes of books letting them drop to the floor. The phones were ringing – customers were demanding service – the stacks of paperwork grew tall.

How I loved books…fiction, non-fiction…any kind, it didn't really matter. Its smell, its feel, the touch of books stacked at my bedside…knowledge waiting to be consumed. At one point, I brought so many books home that my husband pleaded with me not to buy anymore. "There's just no more room in this house!" he complained. So I resorted to sneaking them in late at night, removing them from their noisy paper bags before reaching the door. Yes – going into the bookstore business had been the only thing left to do.

There were special times in the store like late at night and first thing in the morning when no one else was there. I'd walk up and down each aisle, carrying a stick of incense, its trail of smoke curling around each book, blessing the space they filled.

While I was alone, I would just stare at all the rows of books – each written by some known or unknown hand – each bearing a message of its own. It was as if I could hear a thousand voices pleading, "Read me! No, read *me…stay with me awhile!*" I often wondered if that was how our patrons felt when they walked about. I wondered what it was that drew the reader to a specific title amongst so many thousands. Is it that one book's voice that cries out louder than the rest? Why would one go through row after row with no more than a mere glance, then suddenly stop? What mysterious force compels one to stay, to focus in, and then lift a hand trustingly, and unknowingly open a book to the exact words their Soul had longed to hear?

Through the years, I watched this invisible force at work. Like clockwork, a stranger would come into the store on a particular day and I would have a particular book, set on a shelf at a certain hour. Everything lined up. And when it did, that's when I knew I was truly a witness to Divine Order – destined to watch as others reached epiphanies that transformed and changed their lives. How I secretly longed to be as divinely guided as they – swept away by this very same force that compelled the fortunate ones to their true fate.

So here I sat in the office of my own store – Alexandria II in Pasadena, California (co-owned with my nephew Ralph). We had named it after the Alexandrian Library of ancient Egypt where the greatest works on philosophy, alchemy, magic, hermetics, science, and literature were gathered, stored, and written. For ten years I toiled in my own meager way trying to live up to its name. And I felt proud for it had become a haven filled with the hidden teachings and mysteries of all ages – secrets of the great mystics of the past, kept hidden – buried within the pages of their books as anagrams, symbols and art; buried because it was well known, by any avid alchemist or metaphysician, that the student *had to earn* the understanding of this great hidden knowledge. Yes, *this* was my passion – that and an extraordinary need to understand the nature of God.

Meeting Margaret

Enough! My neck ached from hours of catalogs and lifting heavy boxes. I didn't even realize how tired I was until I looked at the clock – it was hours longer than I should have stayed.

As I left my office and entered the store a heavy bag of books was suddenly thrust into my hands, "Would you mind helping this woman to her car?"

The abruptness of the clerk startled me – she had never done this before. I quickly looked up to see an elderly Rubenesque looking woman with something distinctly familiar in her presence. "Not at all," I said, preparing to escort her out. As we looked at one another, her gentle yet intense gaze never wavered.

Just then a young woman came forward, holding more bags. "She's with me – I'm Ruth, and this is Margaret," motioning towards the elderly woman beside her. "She's from Amsterdam and there aren't many stores like this in her country. And as you know, American books are always more expensive overseas."

After briefly chatting with Ruth, we started for her car. But the further we walked along, the stronger I felt compelled to communicate with Margaret – I finally blurted out some question about my health – Ugh, I thought, why couldn't I have said something more profound?

"Why would you think that I would know?" Margaret asked, surprised.

"I'm not sure, I just sensed it."

As Margaret stood there staring into my eyes, I glanced at Ruth who smiled knowingly – as if something magical was about to happen.

"When is your birthday?" Margaret asked.

September 26th, I answered.

She paused, "And the place and time of birth?"

"I'm not sure, there wasn't a time written on my birth certificate," I answered.

There was a much longer pause.

"Give me some important dates, like a marriage, or birth of a child, graduation things like that."

I thought for a moment as she pulled a pencil and paper from her bag. Then answered her the best I could. As she wrote down the dates, she occasionally looked away, calculating the information in her mind.

Just then my husband Chuck approached. After introducing him, Margaret asked the same questions. Obviously, she was interested in our astrological signs, but why? Just as she was getting into the car, she stopped, "There is something...would it be possible to see you both tomorrow?"

My husband and I looked at one another, surprised by the invitation. "Of course," we thought. And after agreeing to see each other again, she was off.

The next day at the store passed quickly. I was excited when the intercom finally sounded with the announcement that Margaret had arrived.

Following greetings, Margaret, Chuck, and I sat at a small table set up in the corner of the office where we silently watched Margaret pull a batch of papers from her bag. She continued to separate the sheets of paper into two neat piles on the table in front of each of us...I took a quick glance at mine.

"You're an astrologer!"

"Well actually, I'm a psychologist, but most people know me for my work in astrology," she explained, pulling her own notes from her bag. "I've drawn the charts for some of the most prestigious royal families of Europe. I've done this all my life."

As I studied the mysterious lines and symbols of my chart, I wished I could have understood what they meant. Astrology was one of those things that I really wanted to study, but never found time to learn. I'd never seen my chart before, and with my untrained eye, it looked rather lop-sided. Where the symbols of Chuck's planets were neatly arranged throughout the twelve segments of his chart, my symbols were clustered within only three segments, lying at the top. This worried me...and she must of known.

"It's actually the perfect chart for you!" she laughed, then continued to calculate Chuck's chart as if she were doing his taxes. Then finally she put the pencil down and looked Chuck seriously in the eyes, "I see that your father had committed suicide."

I looked at her blankly, too stunned for words. And Chuck, though generally outspoken, just blinked dumbstruck, "How could you know?"

"It's right here where the planet…"

Margaret went on explaining the things she saw, then moving from one chart to the other, revealed our past to such precision, I thought a close friend might have counseled her. Our present and future were laid before us as she described his music, our health and opportunities, as well as things to avoid. She gave us advise on parenting, warning us to give our youngest daughter the freedom to play.

I was wondering when she would give me insight into my spiritual life, when suddenly, as if reading my mind, she began…"Because of the configuration of almost all your planets set within these three top areas of your chart, your fate will lead you to find those things which are hidden, be it in text, within the earth, or stars…it doesn't really matter. Wherever you are, the mysteries are bound to you – seeking you out when they are ready to be revealed."

These cryptic words shook my peace – I wondered, what treasures could possibly be left, for me to find.

Meeting Marie

We were amazed that three hours had past. It was time to take Margaret home. She had been staying with Marie Bauer Hall, wife of the late Manly P. Hall, the world-renowned metaphysician and philosopher. After Manly's bizarre death, a mutual friend had generously sent Margaret from Amsterdam, to console Marie with the difficulties of her loss.

By the time we had gotten Margaret back to Marie's, it was nearly midnight and the rain had begun to pour. As we pulled into the driveway, I noticed Margaret's face deepen with concern.

"Marie will be quite upset with me about vanishing the way I did. Perhaps I should have called?"

Vanishing? I thought. Hadn't she explained to Marie where she was going? Now *I* was nervous!

When the car stopped, my heart started beating, as fast as the rain hitting the roof of the car. I just didn't understand why I was feeling so uneasy. As I escorted Margaret up the dark walkway, the wind and rain pounded against our faces. I could barely make out the lines of a Spanish-style home – two sets of tiered stairs led up to its door.

After walking up the first set, I could see a small Japanese teahouse accented by Oriental-designed decorative shrubs, giving it a Zen-like appearance. It was all so peculiarly arranged – a Spanish style home, yet most everything around it had a Japanese design to it…including the mailbox and railing.

As I climbed the second set of steps, we passed a large bay window with Shojis parted open in the middle. As I peeked inside, I could see a fireplace with a magnificent portrait hanging above. The room was illuminated by a soft, dim light, which embraced the silhouette of a small, slender figure that walked stoically towards the door.

There was something eerie about this place. I was glad Margaret went ahead of me, dreading to be the one standing there when Mrs. Hall opened the door.

Just as I was thinking this, the door suddenly burst open. Although the light was dim, I could hardly believe my eyes. Margaret had told me that Marie was ninety years old, but there stood a petite woman looking no older than sixty. Her regal posture and slim figure were accentuated by an elegantly embroidered African dress. Large dangling earrings framed her soft, pale face that looked radiant, almost transparent, with very little signs of aging. Her eyes were dark, yet even in the dim light of the doorway I could see the fire in them.

"Mrs. Hall?" My voice cracked. Margaret walked - no, ran quickly past Marie through the door without even saying a word - leaving me standing there *alone!* As Mrs. Hall looked me straight in the eyes, a flash of lighting lit up the sky. It was like an old movie, the giant bolt rumbling through the air around me — the thunder adding drama to my already anxious scene.

I fumbled with my umbrella nervously. Her voice finally broke the silence as I struggled to hear her over the pouring rain, "Do you know what time it is?"

"I'm sorry, I know it's late, it's just that...." I fumbled for words, quickly excused myself, and then walked briskly to the car.

As I closed the car door behind me, my husband asked, "Well, did you meet her?"

"Yes – and I wouldn't study with her..." I stopped abruptly, recounting what I had just said.

"What do you mean study?"

"I...I don't know why I said that." It *really* didn't make sense. Why would I assume this woman had anything to teach?

Just then I had a feeling I'd forgotten something, as if I was there to pick something up, not to drop someone off. I was experiencing *déjà vu* – sitting there in the dark of night, listening to the rain hitting the roof of the car, thinking of the stranger at the door. Driving off, I was compelled to take one last look at the house and oddly enough, Marie was still standing outside her door. The way the light shone behind her made her silhouette aglow. The image remained in my mind as we drove away.

The First Door

The phone rang early the next morning. I hurried to pick up the receiver before it woke everyone in the house...the voice sounded excited.

"Good morning, this is Margaret – Marie has asked to meet with you and your husband this afternoon. Would you happen to be available?"

"Victoria? Victoria?"

I was still half asleep, but not so dazed as to forget what had happened the night before. I didn't know what to think. What had Margaret said about us? Was it something she'd seen in my chart? I was fearful, yet strangely exhilarated at the thought of meeting Marie again. I took a deep breath, "Sure, that would be fine..."

That afternoon, we drove to Marie's home where Margaret proudly escorted us in. Hanging just outside the entry was a life-size portrait of a young Manly P. Hall – with his deep set eyes, fixed in such an intense glare – I imagined his spirit, resting within the painting, guarding his domain.

From the moment that I entered, it felt as if I'd gone back in time. Like a museum, authentic ancient scrolls flanked beautiful rare Oriental objects in glass cases. Egyptian sculptures, thousands of years old, unpretentiously rested near the window, where delicate Shoji screens lay in place of drapery.

As we walked through the house, my husband and I stopped to take a closer look at a large gold-framed painting, hanging over an oversized Mediterranean fireplace.

"It's Marie," Margaret whispered.

"She was thirty-nine when it was painted."

That was exactly my age.

14

    The painting was spectacular. Marie's dark hair accentuated her pearly white skin reminding me of the actress Vivien Leigh in the movie *Gone with the Wind*. In the portrait, she wore a beautiful red dress with a serpent bracelet coiled about her delicate wrist.

My husband chuckled.

"What?" I asked.

"Look!" There was a small metal sign, gently pushed into the corner of the picture frame. It read: "Caution: High Voltage!" "Her son placed it there as a young boy, and Marie never removed it," Margaret explained.

As we continued to follow Margaret toward the sitting room, we walked through an archway framed by two of the grandest Chinese Foo-dog sculptures I'd ever seen – the shiny porcelain and vibrant colors made them appear life-like; I was sure they were relics from some obscure temple. We were led to a large glass table with wicker chairs. The wallpaper made from bamboo, and the large glass doors overlooking the grounds, made me feel like I was seated in a Japanese garden.

But in spite of all its beauty, there was a sad stillness about this place…it seemed to languish within an almost death-like embrace, as if nothing was allowed to move forward…like something – some force – wanted everything to stay the same. I was in the midst of these thoughts when Marie walked in.

All at once I found my body relax, as this spry, cheery, energetic ninety-year-old woman entered to greet us – a stark contrast to the house itself. Her smile was dazzling. There was no sign of the discomfort that I had experienced with her the night before. She wore an exotically embroidered Latin American dress, with peasant sleeves falling perfectly around her small thin frame. I drew my eyes to the large, dangling, jade earrings that accented her wavy dark hair – they made a soft tinkling noise as she walked.

At first, we spoke casually about the store and ourselves. However, when Marie rose to get us tea, Margaret suddenly leaned forward and whispered in my ear, "Don't mention Marie's husband Manly. She's having a very difficult time dealing with his death."

I could hear Marie working in the kitchen, as Margaret moved in closer, lowering her voice as she went on to explain,

"Manly was a great philosophical author, writing more than one-hundred books; he built a spiritual organization called the Philosophical Research Society, which became world renown..."

I was familiar with this place, passing it each time I drove down Los Feliz; you couldn't miss it. A giant Egyptian pharaoh kneels right smack at the corner of the lot – its imposing sight, looms over the cars that are inevitably forced to stop at its busy intersection. Yet here I sat in the founder's own home, only to find that its sound and serene appearance was only a facade.

As I learned from Margaret, a few years before, some unscrupulous individuals that took advantage of Manly and Marie had infiltrated his organization...and seized control of both the center and their personal possessions. For three years Marie had been consumed within a legal battle to reclaim their properties, and each time the case is about to be closed, the final decision has been stalled. The impact of Manly's death, alongside, years of uncertainty regarding the outcome of her case, had taken its toll on her nerves.

In hearing of Marie's desperate situation, I couldn't help feeling sorry for her, particularly because it had been alleged that these same people might have been involved with Manly's own death.

"Quite sadly, more allegations were raised that the same group had sabotaged the computer in which she placed her work."

"Her work?"

"Yes, she's a Seer," Margaret said. "She's been recording her visions for more than 60 years."

"You mean she's psychic?"

"I've never heard her use that word to describe herself."

Margaret went on to explain that Marie had shown her a diagram that she had drawn of the Garden of Eden. Marie had discovered that a direct message from Eve was being transmitted, and believed that she was to help in its *lawful release...it was the holy unveiling of the history and future of mankind.*

Marie had been shown that Adam and Eve (the foundation of subsequent archetypes for the generations to come) were the only two of our collective to have had true access to the history of Eden – because they were the only ones living to absorb those memories within their Souls. These Soul memories were what Marie referred to as experienced-distilled understanding, understanding gained through personal experience.

Margaret hesitated as if trying to put it in her best words. What she was trying to convey, was that Marie, like Nostradamus, had been given visions – revealing a complete cosmogony – a model of the origins and causes of the universe, its workings and its end. In 1938, Marie began recording these visions in writing, continuing untiringly until the mysterious death of her husband in 1990.

As I sat there, curious to know more, Marie re-entered carrying the tea. She intuitively began a discourse, as if she had been reading our minds. Yet I knew there was simply no way she could have heard us.

"My work, is what I call my *Life's Assignment,*" Marie said...I noticed that her breathing began to slow, and as she began to relax, her eyes seemed to glaze over, as if looking out into some distant past:

A person's Life Assignment is an obligation to life that *must* be fulfilled. It is our true purpose, somewhat like a ship, designed to take us to our destiny. There is no peace unless you are fulfilling your Life's Assignment, for there is an unquenchable thirst – an emptiness and longing – that only *it* can fulfill. Though it may not yet be revealed, your Life's Assignment lies waiting in the innermost recesses of the human spirit – its drama, "this Histo-tragic-comedy of Life," waits to unfold. Its presence is undeniable; its patience unlimited – until you take your first humble step, and then with that step, the pattern within you is ignited. You are filled by a sudden thrust of energy and stamina to complete the task at hand, for this is the *Divine energy of Life* that molds our being, as we are swept away, driven to our destiny.

I knew exactly what she meant by a Life's Assignment...I understood the process by now. After years of searching, I had attuned myself to seeing the magnetic web that had suddenly evolved before me – drawing the people and places necessary for the completion of my own task at hand.

I had long sought the *Mystic's Path*, but now I understood the way. Because our life's assignment is the *path*...leading us to our fate – that one obligation in life that formulates the experiences meant to transform and carry us to our destiny. And somehow, I felt Marie had something to do with mine.

At that moment the doorbell rang. I took a deep breath of disappointment...I wanted to hear more of her thoughts. Marie left us briefly then reentered the room with a tall, slim man. He was handsomely dressed with a neatly cut white beard and mustache that only appeared to accentuate his warm smile.

"I'd like you all to meet Fred Cole," Marie said. "He's a very close friend of mine whom I've known for 43 years."

"I didn't mean to intrude," said Fred apologetically, "but I was on my way home and decided to stop by for a moment."

As Marie continued the introductions I glanced over at Fred. It was clear to see by the gleam in his eyes how dedicated he was to Marie. Fred, as I went on to learn, had played an intricate role in supporting her work throughout the forty-three years they had known one another.

"Did you tell them how you met Manly?" Fred asked.

Marie paused a moment, then smiled. "It was Manly who introduced me to the world that led me to my work. That's where I found my *own* Life's Assignment."

"It was 1934. I was in New York City…"

As she spoke, her eyes gleamed with renewed energy. Her arms and hands flew about as if painting some invisible picture she hoped for us to see. How she loved sharing the secrets of her past:

"…I had just finished shopping in the city and was running terribly late for my train-ride home. Hurrying as fast as I could, I arrived just as the train was leaving the station. I tried to squeeze through the gate, but the stationmaster stood in my way, and refused to let me go by. I pleaded with him to pass, but it was to no avail. He just walked away, leaving me standing there alone – listening to the train make its way over the tracks as it left."

"As I stood there, on the platform," Marie continued, "a stranger approached me. I hadn't even seen him enter the station. He was a well-dressed man, wearing a dark brown suit with a matching brown derby. And he was holding a beautifully carved black-ebony cane. He just walked right up to me and asked, "How long would I be waiting for the next train?"

"I told him, *'a whole hour* – and there isn't even a store open!' The stranger smiled at this, and proposed a lecture, going on at the Pythian Temple nearby."

"Did you ask him who he was?"

"No, I didn't think of it. In fact, I didn't even ask who was speaking at the lecture. I just thanked him for the idea and went off to see for myself and never saw him again."

Fred chimed in excitedly; you could tell he had heard this story many times before, "By the time Marie got there, the auditorium was so crowded, that she could barely squeeze through. The only room she could find to stand was in the balcony over-looking the stage."

"That's where I first saw Manly," Marie broke in, "A stately man sitting beneath a beacon of light, in a magnificent chair that looked like a throne. He was lecturing at the front of this grand hall. His engaging voice never wavered, as his audience stood silent in the darkness – inspired by his ideas. They knew it was his final speaking engagement in New York and they clung to his every word."

As Marie stood within the crowd, pressed against the railings, she felt an immediate attraction for this man, "I couldn't help feeling, I'd known him before; and the more he spoke, the more fascinated I became. "

When Manly finished talking about the mysteries of the ages, he began showing the crowd of people some architectural plans for a future Philosophical Research Society he was to build in Los Angeles. And as Marie would learn, it was to have a library, lecture hall, and a school, which was well suited for her young son.

"When the lecture ended, I was milling out with the crowd when I felt someone grab me by the arm. I looked up to see Manly, a large blue-eyed giant, 6'3" man, looking down at my 5'3" frame."

"I can't recall his first words," Marie confessed, "but I clearly remember him saying, 'Young Lady, you should study the *Secret Doctrine!*'[2] I didn't know what he was talking about at the time. But deep inside I knew he was speaking my language."

Fred stated: "Manly was a very interesting man. He had become a famous philosopher and an ardent collector of rare books, stamps, and Eastern art. He was a 33rd Degree Mason[3] and a member of the Inner Council, using his influence to buy and have access to the world's most secretive works in alchemy,

---

[2] Secret Doctrine: 2 volume book by theosophist, Madame Blavatsky.
[3] Mason: member of a secret fraternal society called the Freemasons.

magic, hermetics, and religion. Where Manly had mastered deciphering these philosophical and esoteric literary works of the past...Marie had mastered an inner world, a true seer unhampered by the limitations of three-dimensional space and time."

Over the years, Fred had come to realize, that it was through this unique perspective that Marie could see, a world within which the mysteries of nature unfold – deciphering the codes and principles of wisdom that seemed to be embedded within the patterns underlying all that existed in the universe. But there was more to these patterns than just extruding its wisdom. What she was able to do was tap into the intelligence that had organized the patterns themselves...finding access to the process through which they were made.

"You make me sound like one of those Eastern masters..." Marie broke in, "and in order to be a master, you've got to have willing or unwilling slaves. And as far as I'm concerned, I certainly don't want to be a guru who reaches enlightenment, and then floats off to Nirvana leaving the dirt behind for the rest of us to clean up! No...we're in this together."

Marie then leaned over to me smiling, and said, "You see, God made man to devise secrets. Then he changed his mind and created woman to break them wide open."

And that's exactly what she did. I felt Life's veil of secrecy suddenly torn apart and a shift of energy hit the room like a bolt of lightening. We all sat there in awe.

The language Marie used to reveal her message was strange, yet familiar, undecipherable, alluring. Her words seemed to reverberate within my Soul and my Natural Mind.[4]

We began to experience a shift in consciousness – a quiet peace took over the room. As she spoke, it was as if the Universe

---

[4] Natural Mind: the mind of our physical form (backed by a brain). We have 3 minds working in different dimensions, Natural Mind, Spiritmind, and Soulmind.

was stripped open wide. We were mesmerized...as she went on, I felt tears in my eyes.

Frozen in time, caught in the hypnotic sound of her voice, I was absorbed into a state of ecstasy. The knowledge of our origins and causes lay stretched before me. There it was, *before* any world was...a dark love-warmth...a living Intelligence whose nature is a love-awareness...spread like a blanket, filling all of space. Its alive...breathing! I know it's breathing because I felt its breath as mine – it was keeping *me* alive. This Intelligence was aware I was there! I was like a child allowed a glimpse. I could see – even if only for those few, brief moments – I watched as the cosmos danced before me.

Where was I? How did Marie do this? My mind had gone beyond our conscious knowing, into a world of what felt like pure understanding...a solid and complete state of awareness... Being.

Marie kept on. Her eyes glowed; her face softened with every word. As I watched her speak, the room became transparent. I left my body and natural mind...crossing over...transformed into a world where her words were clear and pure.

As my Soul with its memories was summoned, I lost all sense of self. Her sweet words were like golden pearls spiraling out from some dark, unknown abyss of my mind - filling a void so deep within me, and a hunger so vast – that each syllable uttered became food for my Soul:

> *I heard her, but not with ears...*
> *I sensed her thoughts, beyond my mind.*
> *I could see, but not with mortal eyes...*
> *She spoke of the Causal Mother, the Trinity,*
> *and the Mystery of the Number Four...*
> *the Virgin Soul, the search for the Holy Grail...*
> *First Energy, and the Birth of Eternal Time.*

Suddenly, like hearing an echo from the past, I awoke to hear her familiar voice whispering, "Let hang on what may…all this will be said again."

I felt paralyzed, then shuddered as I blinked my eyes, trying to bring myself back from the trance-like state. My memory was still unclear, "What did she say?"

What were those words?

What had she said about Time?

I had so many questions.

Staring deeply into my eyes, Marie broke the silence, "Don't worry…though your Natural Mind may not understand the things you have seen and heard your Soulmind has absorbed it all. You see the Divine Pattern within your Soul has been ignited. Within these lines of Life and light, lies a Universal Intelligence that connects us to the very same intelligence that lies within the patterns of *all life* and *all living*. This intelligence carries ancient memories, collected before time itself. And once your physical and spirit *Patterns of Life* have been realigned to the pattern of the Soul, you awaken these memories that gradually become a part of you again. You will begin to recognize the deeper meanings of things; for truth is eternal, familiar; it is embedded within the essence of all that exists."

A strange shiver ran through my body as I became aware that I might be in the presence of someone who had *finally* unlocked the door to the secrets of Life. Glancing from the corner of my eye, I noticed that my husband too had come under the spell of this surreal unfolding. Could it be that she was either knowingly or unknowingly initiating us into the depths of some mystery?

I turned to ask a question, but noticed it had become dark outside. I didn't know how long we'd been there, but Marie looked tired. As I got to my feet, I felt a heightened sense of awareness, clarity marked by a lightness of being. She had skillfully reconnected us and I soon became aware that my husband and I were the only ones left with Marie in the room.

We stood there silent as Marie handed us a few of her books then placed a smaller book on the top of the heap. "These are the *Sonnets of GSO,*[5] an obscure collection of Alchemical poetry from the 1930's – it once saved my life." Then wished us a goodnight.

Chuck and I walked to the car in silence trying to make sense of it all. I was so grateful that I wasn't alone.

"It was unbelievable," I whispered in a daze, "did you hear what I heard?

"I'm not sure what exactly happened, or what she said, but there was something in it that seemed to make me feel at peace."

He was right...I too felt that peace. And somehow, in a deeper sense or intuitively, I understood all those strange words she used – yet consciously, I felt confused. She was using familiar words in unfamiliar ways. Magically, her use of language functioned to evoke a deeper sense to its meaning. I didn't find its mystique daunting at all. In fact, this only drew me closer to the work.

I lay in bed that night powerless to stop my thoughts. What I had encountered that day was not the knowledge coming from the *outside,* as through books – no, this was a true experience that suffers the heat, then ignites the essence of our being – bringing with it a distilled understanding or wisdom that comes from *within.* I couldn't help wondering what it was that allowed me to reach this altered state of being. And more importantly, what was at the heart of Marie's Cosmogony that seemed to resonate with my Soul?

---

[5] Unknown author. Works compiled by Walter Owen.

As I lay there reading through her works, I realized that Marie wasn't asking me to completely abandon myself to blind faith. I found a spiritual logic to her work that made it feel safe to believe. The more I read, the more I could see that the earmarks of its essence lie embedded within the core of many other beliefs I had studied over the years. Yet somehow, deep inside I knew that here within her pages this essence would finally be defined.

I was on a quest – to understand the nature of the Divine. I didn't believe that God was the "unknowable," because I had awakened – and the search had now become my reason for living. Now, I was sure of what I had come for...the Cosmogony:

> *I had been given a glimpse at the light of Truth*
> *and found a living, breathing, love-intelligence –*
> *only to be humbled by Wisdom's breath*
> *and the depth of its love.*

But what was I to do? I wanted more than a glimpse. I had meditated for hundreds of hours, but few times had I come to this kind of profound understanding. How I'd longed to remember her every word.

The next day, we were invited to return. Armed with a tape recorder and pad, we began our search for the origins of our Soul – the Holy Grail. And I would soon discover, that its unveiling was the Mystery of the Number Four – not through Buddhism, Taoism, Islam, or Judaism, but through her visions and writings – encompassing mystic Christianity, Rosicrucianism, Alchemy, and True Masonry, whose faces had long been hidden from my sight.

Fifty Years of Work

Marie showed us around. Boxes, boxes, and more boxes filled with papers. I'd never seen anything like it! Did she ever stop writing? When did she sleep? We walked through the house and found more piles of delicate pages browned with age. She showed us the storage shed filled with more of the same. Papers were everywhere, some water damaged, some half eaten by silverfish – all in total disarray. But there, lying half-hidden among the clutter, sat three small boxes that were neatly tied shut. Marie saw me looking at them and opened one up. "Fred wrapped these years ago," she explained "They're my original manuscripts."

The manuscripts lay neatly stacked one upon the other. The pages were yellowed and crinkled and a few were held together by a mere piece of yarn. My fingers tingled as I gently thumbed through the meticulously typed manuscripts. It was exciting just reading the titles aloud, "The 47th Proposition, The Birth of Eternal Time, Origins of the Fourth Dimension, Beginnings of the Human Race." They were like gems in my hands. I struggled to resist my impatience. If allowed, I would have pulled up a chair and started reading them right there.

These manuscripts had sat untouched for years left to deteriorate, buried and discounted. But to *me,* this body of work appeared as illuminated manuscripts, forgotten in caves like the Dead Sea Scrolls.

I smiled to myself, looking at the stacks of papers, realizing that this was no accident, my being here. There was no doubt in my mind that the very same force that had guided others to the books within my store, had finally summoned me...and I understood why...it was because of the nature of my work.

I was a bookseller, and had grown used to the mountainous stacks and piles of paperwork and books that surrounded me for so many years. I had learned to quickly assess the high volumes of materials, reorganizing and sorting them for distribution throughout the store. However, more importantly, I was simply set to the task of disseminating material. And now that I was being called, it was perfectly clear: I was to archive, disseminate and preserve this work, which might otherwise be lost to a more tenebrous fate.

Marie slowly turned to us, smiling, "I have more to show you."

We followed her through the kitchen. "It's in here," she said, turning the old-fashioned key to unlock the basement door.

I was aroused by curiosity. What was so important that it was kept down here?

"The Light (truth)
Descended into the Darkness (minds of men)...
But the Darkness(minds) Knew It Not."
(didn't recognize it)

She cautioned us to watch our step, as we descended the old and creaky stairwell into the darkness below. Our excited voices echoed through the air and the smell of dank earth penetrated our senses as if entering some buried chamber. The dim light revealed a long narrow eerie hallway that twisted its way toward a small room hidden from our sight. The ancient Egyptian tapestries that hung casually on the walls welcomed us, as if they were maps to this tunnel descending into the Earth.

Upon reaching the bottom of the stairs, I noticed a small door hidden beneath the stairwell. The door was slightly ajar, so as the others went on ahead, I decided to find out what was behind it. I slowly pushed it opened, remembering Marie had mentioned Bela Lugosi would frequently come to visit. Because it was dark and empty, it reminded me of one of his old movies where a monster would pop out at any time.

After peering past the door I saw, what looked to be, hundreds of delicate spider webs glistening in the light – enshrouding piles of paper as though protecting them from the paper-eating predators, thereby extending their life. Strange, I thought – how fate is…even the spiders had done *their* job. As I stood there, I began to feel as though I were being watched – so I quickly closed the door behind me, and rejoined the others up ahead.

As we continued to the last room at the end of the gloomy hall, a feeling of excitement filled the air. The switch was turned on and the small bulb that lit the room, combined with the sunlight peering through the tiny window of the basement, cast an ethereal light. Marie walked to the corner of the room where a large, flat, gray, metal cabinet (the kind used by architects to store their blueprints) sat on a large, heavy wooden platform.

Tightening her small hands around its glistening handles, she hesitated, then carefully pulled open, the first of five drawers. It felt as if she were opening a tomb…a strange, intense and powerful energy flooded the room, reverberating in my Soul.

As we moved in closer, our eyes opened wide with amazement. On 25" X 30" boards she had drawn what she called, *Geometrically True **Diagrams*** – it felt like I was looking into a thousand mandalas: Ⓤ

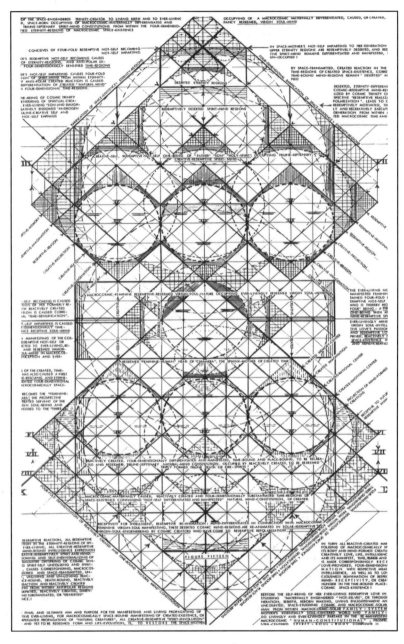

Existence Ⓤ

Its energy was hypnotic – each line, circle, and shape were hand-drawn, curiously balanced, one element evolving into the next. They were so precise one would think a fine architect had done them. Yet this was no work of an ordinary architect.

"Within these drawings are the basic patterns underlying the structure of our living universe," Marie said as she pointed to the diamond shaped lines that lay within intricate squares, "these lines of light are like veins, that carry life and intelligence into form."

I would eventually come to learn, that Marie's visions were not always pictures of objects, but living patterns within the make-up of the objects themselves. These patterns, she explained were magnetic-like webs of Life and light intelligence that was embedded within all forms on all dimensions. By working with the diagramming of these patterns, it evoked further visions – that would unveil the multi-dimensional worlds of existence.

"These darker circles represent cosmic entities, along with their stages of involution and evolution – here we can see Soul division and incarnation," she said pointing to the dotted lines and circles."

"One of these drawings," she explained, "shows how the astrological symbols took their form."

Lifting the first diagrammatic board, I saw another, then another. The drawer was filled to the top. I opened the second drawer then the third, and on, and found all five drawers filled – there seemed to be more than a hundred of them.

As I stared into the intricately detailed drawings, a peculiar hunger to understand them began to ache in my Soul.

"Did you draw these?"

"Oh, Yes. It was 1940 – I saw things in a childlike way and would kind of tune in, maybe not to God, but to how God might look at things. I was radically determined at the time, and when the visions began, the diagramming was a place to help me focus all that intensity. It helped to make things clear – this was the only way I could explain some of the things I saw."

31

"Marie?" A familiar voice called out, jolting us from our reverie as footsteps moved down the stairway toward us.

"Fred? Is that you?

"Yes, it's me. What are you all doing down here?"

"I'm showing them the diagrams," Marie answered.

I watched as Fred entered and hugged Marie affectionately. A smile lit up his face as he looked on proudly, "You know, I got that cabinet from a blueprint shop about ten years ago."

"It's a good thing," Chuck said, pointing to a water stain that flowed down the wall next to the cabinet. "Looks like there was a leak. If the drawings had been left out they could've been destroyed."

Fred turned to Marie, "Do you remember the day your husband had left for work – and when he walked back in, you asked him if he'd forgotten something?"

Turning to us he continued, "Marie had been so engrossed in the diagrams, that she didn't realize nine hours had passed – it was five-o'clock that evening!

"That was about the time my family started to worry about me because of the intensity with which I threw myself into the diagrams. Drawing these patterns was hypnotic – I was held completely spellbound over my drawing board. In fact, I became so absorbed I didn't eat or sleep…I forgot I was alive. That's when it started to cause a heightened ability of extra sensory perception. There was something unearthly strange about drawing these patterns in the order that I had drawn them."

The more she spoke, the more fascinated I became.

"They induced all sorts of things – precognition, tuning into people's thoughts, waking visions. This was something that my family couldn't understand, nor accept. They thought I was going mad. It scared them. It was about that time, I started to think about giving it up, but before I had the good sense to stop, something happened."

Marie hesitated for a moment, "I went into a coma that lasted for weeks."

"The doctors couldn't diagnose the problem," Fred intervened. "They told her family that death was imminent."

"Ah, but this was no ordinary coma" Marie continued as she went to sit comfortably in a chair, "I couldn't move or speak, but there were many times I was coherent and able to hear people talking in my room."

Marie explained, that she felt like a prisoner within her own body, alternating between conscious and unconscious states. No matter how hard she tried, she simply couldn't move or speak. Until one day while lying in the hospital, she finally found a reprieve...she remembered a book about a prisoner of war that used a technique called astral projection[6] to see his family. Marie applied the same method used by the soldier to contact *her* sister – she concentrated on breathing, while focusing on the image of her sister's face. Before long, Marie began to experience a strange trembling-sensation, followed by a feeling that she was slowly rising from her body. Then instantaneously, she was projected to her sister's side – not physically – but as a ghost-like image! And as amazing as it may seem (to those who have never experienced this form of psychic phenomenon) her sister received this startling image, whereby Marie summoned her help. The shocked and frightened woman knew her sister's powers well, and immediately traveled by train to Marie's bedside.

"The moment my sister arrived," Marie explained, "she took hold of my wrist, becoming a conduit for the energy that I simply couldn't muster for myself. And before long, much to everyone's surprise, I was suddenly able to regain consciousness."

At first, Marie's vision was hazy and for a while she relied on her sister's presence rather than muster energy of her own.

---

[6] Astral projection: A technique of leaving the physical body behind, while consciously traveling outside it in what is called an astral body.

"When I walked, I would sort of sway to a beat of some unknown harmony. It took months to readjust." However, in time, she returned to her natural state and never allowed herself to be so consumed by the diagrams again.

Marie, recalling her past, began to warn us of the use of the diagrams, *Geometrically-trued Diagramming* creates a multi-dimensional wave in space, which can influence one's state of consciousness (just as these waves influence matter on all dimensions). "It's mesmerizing. You must be careful not to loose yourself within them."

I looked at the drawing in front of me. There is something about them -- something alluring, and magnetic. They felt familiar and accessible to me. I knew intuitively, that I could somehow understand these mysterious drawings – all I had to do was find the key.

While ascending the stairs back to the kitchen, I was haunted by the images of the drawings. My mind was filled with lines and symbols re-creating its powerful form. This work was too important to be buried in a basement.

I turned to my husband, asking him to work with me in organizing Marie's work. By the time we'd returned to the sitting room, we had both made an important decision that would influence the rest of our lives.

"Marie," I said, feeling awkward, and not knowing how she would respond, "my husband and I have talked it over, and would like to help you organize your life's work. We have..."

Before I could finish the most beautiful smile came across her face. Her body relaxed, as if we had lifted a heavy burden from her back...no, from her Soul. Her bright and intelligent eyes, once tense and concentrated, had been replaced by those filled with a strangely gratified, sense of peace – she had grown old of carrying the work by herself – and I thought, she was finally ready for its *release:*

"It is a work that I have dedicated my life to. I've been awed by it...yet experienced both great joy and sorrow. Every choice you make on this path must be done through humility; for humility is the last thing we learn. Remember, it is both the *intent and intensity* by which you apply yourself to the work, that will decide how deeply you will penetrate its mysteries."

Solve et Coagula:
Break Down to Rebuild

The next morning when Marie opened the door, I relished the look of her surprise – we had decided to take the day off and were standing on her porch with a crew of twenty volunteers.

"I've called on my spiritual militia Marie, to help us organize your work. These are my closest friends."

I was so excited, but not nearly as Marie. She was grinning from ear to ear, extending herself with a warm welcome as everyone crowded into her entry, she embraced each as they gave their name. Anyone would have thought that a compulsive writer like Marie would have panicked at the sight of strangers about to rummage through her papers. Instead, she embraced our efforts, accepting us into her life.

Marie led us through almost every room in the house, turning it upside down, searching for any material that pertained to what I refer to as the Arcanum (Mysteries). And as the items began to mount, I soon discovered that the piles of papers, books, manuscripts and tapes were far more than I had anticipated.

All sorts of things ran through my head as the mountains of materials began to grow. I started to feel overwhelmed while wondering how I was going to organize it all. Where would it be stored?

I started to realize how intimidating this must look for the others and had to think fast. "All right," I called out to everyone, "We're going to have to divide and sort the tapes, books, and pictures into individual rooms. Just like sections within a bookstore."

Each of us grabbed a box or a stack of items, separating them like a mailman on his route. One room resulted in hundreds of tapes, including some of Marie's old lectures on 5" reels. We even found some old wire tapes that had been shoved into the back of an unused drawer.

After awhile, the room filled with paperwork began to look like a paper factory hit by a tornado. Huge stacks of boxes and papers were scattered everywhere. Photocopies of images, found in books dating back to the 14th and 15th century, lay in heaps on the floor. We found thousands of 8½ x 11 printed copies of the diagrams in the basement that now shone amidst the mounds of papers like jewels glittering in the snow. Most were in good condition, except for some ragged, and discolored ends. We salvaged them by cutting the damage away and then numbered them for our files.

Everything was typewritten. And as I went through the stacks, meticulously and delicately handling page by page, I noticed that some were duplicates of the original manuscripts. I thought about it for a moment, and then realized that computers and copy machines weren't available forty years ago. So instead of retyping, Marie had resorted to making four or five carbon copies of anything she was working on. And even after the equipment was available, she just kept on making copies. I could hardly imagine the amounts of paper she must have used.

I would later find that in some instances, the extra copies became essential, especially when no original manuscripts were found. But many of these copies were either damaged or had missing pages and separating them was not an easy task. The paper was so old and brittle that it fell apart in our hands. Luckily, Dorothy Ives, wife of the late performer Burl Ives, had donated a copy machine a year before…if she only knew what a lifesaver it had become.

At this point I decided to join the others who were sitting on the floor separating the sheets by subject or title. I reached into a stack.

"Ouch…something bit me!"

I slowly sifted through the sheets with a pencil, when I noticed something catch the light. It may have been its eyes. Taking my pencil I carefully lifted another sheet…only to reveal a straight pin sticking up into the air. What was *this* doing in here?

As I combed through the pages, I started to find straight-pins everywhere. At closer examination, I realized that anytime Marie typed a correction for her manuscripts, rather than typing it over, she would use a straight pin to attach the sheet. I had found out that Marie was a great seamstress, and can only assume she decided to employ the same techniques to her office work. We couldn't replace these pins, because tape, over time, damaged the paper even more. So from here on, every time we dove into a stack of papers, we had to watch not to be stabbed!

While the others were busy with the sorting of paperwork, photographs, mail, and other items, I went to check on my nephew, the computer genius in the family, who was working on Marie's computer. I noticed there was a problem, and for a while, sat there peering over his shoulders worrying about what treasures may have been lost and uttering silent prayers.

In the final phase of her work, Marie had integrated computer technology. The entire body of her fourth book was just completed when the system's hard-drive failed. She suspected someone from the PRS had mysteriously tampered with it. And because she had no copies of the database, she didn't know if she could ever retrieve those years of work. It would take days for Greg to rebuild the system, and another week before retrieving the information.

The basement was the last room we went through, and with out central air-conditioning, it was warm and stuffy. The moment I entered the back room, the large metal cabinet filled with the mysterious diagrams beckoned me. The temptation to study its contents was strong, but there was so much to do. And peering at the diagrams would only take up valuable time I didn't have. To decipher its contents would have to wait. I had to be prepared, ready…the timing had to be right.

As I stood there for a moment trying to figure out where to begin, I noticed a few boxes that appeared as though purposely tucked from sight. They were buried beneath some bags of clothing lying in a corner of the room.

I called out to Chuck to help me pull the boxes out. They were heavy, jammed into a corner and difficult to move. Together we lifted one onto a table. "Bruton," was written on each of its sides. Anxiously we opened the box, letting the old, rotting tape fall apart in our hands. Removing the delicate tissue that covered its contents, we discovered old newspaper clippings dated 1938.

"Look at this," I said, holding the delicate, yellowed sheets up for Chuck to see, "The Search for Bruton Vault."

As I continued to read the article, Chuck rummaged through the box. "Here's a picture of a graveyard," reading the description, "A vault had been buried in a small churchyard in

Williamsburg, Virginia…and according to the article, it was a code discovered on the tombstones, that led them to the vault."

The box contained more pictures, strange maps of gravesites and tracings made from tombstones with anagrams written on brittle, yellowed paper. There were newspaper articles, books, geophysical surveys, and old telegrams speaking of codes and treasures:

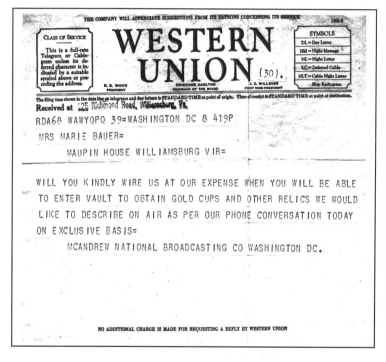

WILL YOU KINDLY WIRE US AT OUR EXPENSE WHEN YOU WILL BE ABLE TO ENTER VAULT TO OBTAIN GOLD CUPS AND OTHER RELICS WE WOULD LIKE TO DESCRIBE ON AIR AS PER OUR PHONE CONVERSATION TODAY ON EXCLUSIVE BASIS =
MCANDREW NATIONAL BROADCASTING CO WASHINGTON DC.

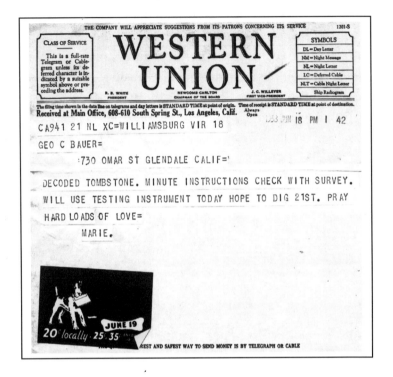

DECODED TOMBSTONE. MINUTE INSTRUCTIONS
CHECK WITH SURVEY. WILL USE TESTING
INSTRUMENT TODAY HOPE TO DIG 21ST. PRAY
HARD LOADS OF LOVE =
MARIE (Telegram to Marie's first husband[1].)

As Chuck and I read through the articles, we found references to Sir Francis Bacon, Shakespeare, the Rockefellers, and the Fraternal Order of the Masons.

As I was to learn, the Fraternal Order of the Mason's described in Marie's work, were not the modern day Masons – but the original sect – a secret organization that few modern Masons are made aware of. This mysterious group had based their teachings around ceremonials designed to portray the successive steps or degrees of spiritual attainment. It was believed that through these steps, one would be lead to Self-Mastery – and with Self-Mastery came power over nature itself.

We also found reference to another secret order called the Rosicrucians (circa 1460), a mystical order whose rituals were thought to have descended from the ancient Egyptian Mystery Schools. Their initiations too, were said to reveal the mysteries of life.

As I continued to rummage through the box, a strange looking article with a picture of diggings around tombstones in a cemetery caught my eye. The article read: "Williamsburg was taken aback this summer when a young woman by the name of Mrs. Marie Bauer, armed only with a code and some old manuscripts and books, blew into town and laid siege to Bruton Parish Church." It also spoke of a "Baconian Cipher," an anagrammatic code that Marie had discovered in 1938. There were handwritten notes attached, explaining how Sir Francis Bacon was the true author of the Shakespeare plays, and through his genius, discovered the *Divine Plan of Creation,* the process through which creation returns to Oneness. The notes further explained Bacon's revelation of the Lost Word, and though he believed that the sound of the Lost Word was unutterable, through a process of conditioning the natural mind one could unveil the secrets of nature and acquire the ability to take a thought and manifest it in the natural world.

To protect this secretive process for future generations, Bacon devised a technique through which he and his contemporaries could hide this information – a code that was buried within their own texts as well as within the great *original* Masonic writings. Marie discovered while deciphering the code that a vault had been buried in the graveyard adjacent to Bruton Church. Within it were treasures such as gold and silver, alongside spiritual riches "not of this earth"; and information describing the destiny of America and humanity at large (including commodities most valued in the future). There were also manuscripts of Bacon's Divine Plan, the originals of the Shakespearean plays and the Bible, put into copper cylinders and physically buried in the vault – its contents, duplicated and buried within each principal nation (each vault containing the whereabouts of every other vault.

However, the one vault stressed most, was the one buried beneath the original foundations of Bruton Parish Church in Williamsburg, Virginia. It had been built in 1673, forty-seven years after the death of Sir Francis Bacon, the original designer of "Freemasonry" (though other sects of Masonry did exist).

We were so engrossed with our findings that we hadn't even heard Marie come down the stairs. When she saw what we had found, she immediately became excited, "I've been looking for these," thumbing through the pages, "It happened so long ago."

"Did you ever find this Bruton Vault?" I asked.

She looked up and smiled, "We dug. But of course, we wouldn't have known where to dig, or even that the vault existed, had it not been for the *Wither Book.*"

"*Wither Book?*" I asked.

"Come with me…"

The Mysterious Wither Book

Marie had followed Manly to California where she had relocated her family in hopes that her son would receive the enlightened education the proposed *Philosophical Research Society* (PRS) was to provide.

"It was an exciting time for me," Marie explained, as we carried the boxes up the stairs. "The PRS was just built, and they needed volunteers to help organize the library. It was while working in the library one late afternoon in 1938 that I noticed an old volume sitting on a shelf, outside of its usual encasement. Its edges had been worn and frayed, so it was left out to be rebound at a repair shop, the next day."

Marie stood up, walked over to a large credenza and delicately lifted the actual book from the drawer!

"Let me introduce you to *George **Wither's** Collection of Emblemes, Ancient and Moderne.*"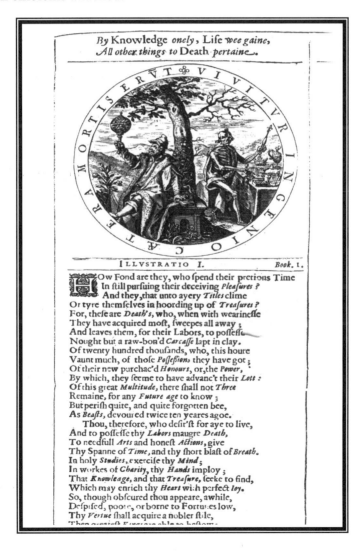

Marie held in her hands, the original copy of the book she had found in 1938. It's deep mustard color looked almost golden. The words EMBLEMES and GeoWITHER were embossed on its cover in gold. The book had been written in 1634 – four books bound into one. The text contained a total of two hundred poems with emblems attached:

By Knowledge *onely*, Life *wee gaine*, *All other things* to Death *pertaine*.

ILLVSTRATIO I.   Book. 1.

Ow Fond are they, who fpend their pretious Time
In ftill purfuing their deceiving *Pleafures* ?
And they, that unto ayery *Titles* clime
Or tyre themfelves in hoording up of *Treafures* ?
For, thefe are *Death's*, who, when with wearineffe
They have acquired moft, fweepes all away ;
And leaves them, for their Labors, to poffeffe
Nought but a raw-bon'd *Carcaffe* lapt in clay.
Of twenty hundred thoufands, who, this houre
Vaunt much, of thofe *Poffeffions* they have got ;
Of their new purchac'd *Honours*, or, the *Power*,
By which, they feeme to have advanc't their *Lott* :
Of this great *Multitude*, there fhall not *Three*
Remaine, for any *Future age* to know ;
But perifh quite, and quite forgotten bee,
As *Beafts*, devoured twice ten yeares agoe.
    Thou, therefore, who defir'ft for aye to live,
And to poffeffe thy *Labors* maugre *Death*,
To needfull *Arts* and honeft *Actions*, give
Thy Spanne of *Time*, and thy fhort blaft of *Breath*.
In holy *Studies*, exercife thy *Mind* ;
In workes of *Charity*, thy *Hands* imploy ;
That *Knowleage*, and that *Treafure*, feeke to find,
Which may enrich thy *Heart* with perfect *Ioy*.
So, though obfcured thou appeare, a while,
Defpifed, poore, or borne to Fortunes low,
Thy *Vertue* fhall acquire a nobler ftile,

*God As Mother*

Marie handed me the rare book, allowing us to thumb through its pages as if looking through a magazine. When she revealed its true purpose: a tool for divination, like tarot or I Ching, I became curious as to its technique.

"First you ask the book a question; then you turn the dial in the back of the book which leads you to a number on a page. Thus, you will find your answer revealed within its 200 poems."

I turned to the back of the book, to see a strange paper dial in the center of a wheel of numbers.

"The strangest thing happened, the first time I opened this book," Marie continued. "There were specific letters that stood out boldly from the page like an illuminated Bible. These letters were either spaced differently within the words; part of misspelled words, or sometimes of a different typeface. It was from here that I first discovered the Code."

I sat there for a moment in disbelief. Not from what she said; but from thinking of all those titles in my bookstore that were reprints of rare manuscripts. Many of them contained editorial comments and apologies for any errors left uncorrected – due to what they assured us to be, "errors in spacing and misspellings" within the original texts.

"Look at this." Marie showed us a picture in the book, and then pulled a few small pieces of delicate tissue paper from the drawer. She began to show us the title page within the Wither Book, then laid the tissue neatly over the page, so that the **anagrams** she had marked on the tissue, would line up with the letters on the page. 🄾

"I began by using tissue paper to trace the strange letters that seemed to stand out on the title page of the *Wither Book*. I looked for misspellings and odd spacing within words, which would generally line up diagonally or in the shape of an X – criss-crossing rows, and sometimes covering the entire page. That's

44

when I noticed there was a tendency for the anagrams to begin at any one of the four corners of a page:

Wither Book: the words "*vault*" and "***William Shakespeare***" 📖

Once I had the pronounced letters, traced on the tissue, I then began drawing lines connecting these letters to form new words. Then, to my surprise these new words formed completely *new* sentences":

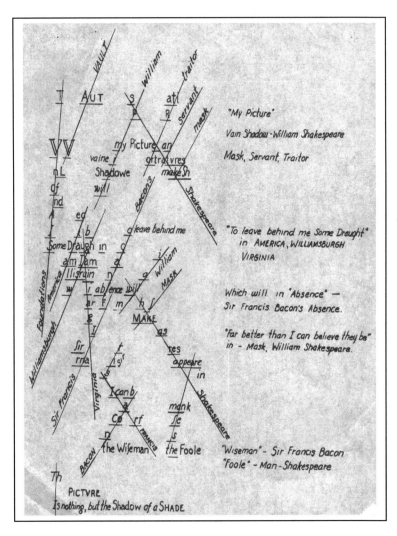

Marie pulled another small piece of yellowed tissue from the back of the book, and laid it over the title page. Here she had outlined the words *"Bacon," "American," "Williamsburg, vault unveiled"* and *"Shakespeare/fool,"* in red.

She then pulled out a poem she had found, and began to decipher its encoded meaning:

Oh blame me not if I no more can write!
(Marie explained: Can't write because the author is dead)
Looke in your glasse and there appeares a face,
(Marie: See your own face in the reflection before you)
That over-goes my blunt invention quite,
(Marie: Rewrites my works or invention [the code])
Dulling my lines, and doing me disgrace.
(Marie: Changing my lines and in doing so, ruining its impact, meaning, and all I had set to do)
Shakespeare Sonnet 103

Marie, as I went on to learn, had found that the emblems in the *Wither Book* contained more than scenarios of life and death. It became evident that their primary focus was churches, tombstones, and a woman digging in cemeteries – always with a church in the background:

This, she explained triggered her imagination. She began to question if the emblems were mere fanciful drawings, or perhaps if they had another intent?

As the group of us peered through the book, we found skulls, hourglasses, and the alchemical symbol of the uroboros[7] – the eternal return. Marie felt that these illustrations symbolized long periods of time.

There were also symbols of hope and abundance signified by cornucopias and horns of plenty, along with drawings depicting a buried treasure, not only physical, but that of spiritual or *True Knowledge* having been buried into vaults and texts.

"Then there was another stunning discovery," Marie continued. "While I thumbed through the pages, I found an inverted emblem that appeared to be printed incorrectly":

---

[7] A snake wound in a circle with its own tail within its mouth.

"I knew that there were two other original copies of the *Wither Book* in Manly's collection and was able to make a definitive comparison."

In that moment, Marie pulled a second and third copy of the *Wither Book* from the drawer and opened them up for us to compare:

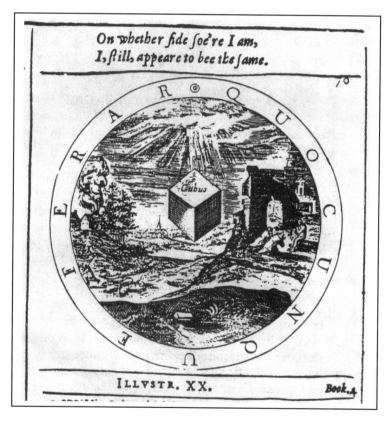

The emblem was correctly placed in the other two copies...the copy she had discovered lying out that day, contained the only error.

"The more I saw of the book, the more fascinated I became. I began to question, why this apparently flawed copy had fallen into my hands?"

In Marie's profoundly analytical mind, she had connected this obscure printing error with a code found within the book – equating the cube, "10 foot square" suspended in mid-air, as a clue to not only the size and shape of the vault, but to the depth in which it was buried within the ground.

At this point, Marie was convinced that there must be a strange force at work drawing her to the information encrypted in the book. She began to find anagrams that described Shakespeare as a "fake," "a rouse," protecting the identity of the true authors – Sir Francis Bacon and his well-known contemporaries (33 in all) – their identities concealed for political reasons. She went on to find that they had encoded this book, as well as other books of their time, and could only assume that when asked to work on the King James Version of the Bible, they may have done the same.

As Marie began investigating the writings of Bacon and his contemporaries, her suspicions were confirmed. She found that encoded messages, symbols and illustrations of **churchyards** and hidden vaults, were characterized throughout *their* work as well.

Manly had entrusted Marie with the valuable manuscript to take home for further study. And through a painstaking process of analyzing the drawings and anagrams, while creating historical links, she came to the final conclusion, that a vault must be hidden in the graveyard of Bruton Church in Williamsburg. But her work was not complete…she still didn't know the exact location to begin the dig.

"The moment had come." Marie said. "One morning in 1938, I showed my findings to Manly, and after a few more weeks of intensive analysis, I realized that the exact location of the vault could only be found near Bruton Church. Therefore, the only thing left for me to do, was to go to Williamsburg myself."

Using her own funds, and asking nothing of Manly, Marie armed with the *Wither Book* struck out on her own, in search of Bruton Vault…leaving her husband and children behind.

50

Part II

Williamsburg

Williamsburg, Virginia

On May 29th 1938, Marie arrived in Williamsburg to find that the Rockefeller Foundation was busy buying up and restoring the historical landmarks, which included a substantial area of the town surrounding Bruton Parish. The buildings and homes were being purchased from the landowners with a stipulation that they would maintain a "life-right" to occupy it.

Block by block, the Rockefeller's research team, architects and builders, would buy and restore each building to what they thought was the original architectural design. But there were a few buildings, that though the Rockefeller's could restore they were *not* allowed to purchase – and among them was Bruton Church. Yet purchasable or not, they were in charge, and it didn't take Marie long to realize that even if she did know where the vault was buried, it would be the Restoration Team that would be doing the digging for the vault. And to get them to do this would require a partnership with the Rockefeller Foundation itself.

When Marie crossed the tiny street to Bruton Parish, she carried the Wither Book tightly under her arm. Standing at the entrance to the churchyard, was like a dream that had become a reality – there stood, the first brick church in Bruton Parish, its tower, a dark silhouette, butted up against the pale blue sky. It was here, according to the cipher, beneath this very tower that the vault was buried.

"One of the first things I noticed was that the tombstone located near the entrance gate had the same coat of arms as shown in the *Wither Book:* three crescent moons. But no sooner had I noted this, that my eyes were drawn to another tomb which read *'Here lyeth the body of **Ann** the wife of **Graham Frank.'** It took me a moment, and then realized that another "a" was lined up under Ann, spelling Anna. Suddenly, I could see, it was the code...Anna-gram!"

"Then, as I looked across the graveyard, I saw something more startling. One of the tombstones had a unique shape that looked very familiar. I quickly opened the *Wither Book* I held in my hands. Thumbing through the pages, as fast as I could, I made a startling discovery...the David Bray Tomb showed a remarkable resemblance to an illustration within my book":

David Bray Tomb

Though **weaknesse** *unto mee belong,*
In my Supporter, *I am strong.*

68

Wither Book

Marie walked over and read the tombstone inscription, and noticed that it was written in Latin – which she later found to be the only tomb written in Latin within the entire graveyard.

"At this point, I wondered if this David Bray had any relation to **Guil Bray**, a signature I found beneath a Latin inscription in the front of the Wither Book." ⏸

Marie then explained how she was later drawn to the James Nicolson tomb, because of its location near the church. Its letters were deeply inscribed into the tombstone and still in good condition. At the center of its epithet, written larger than any of the surrounding text, was the word "Reader." And to Marie, as she explained, there was no doubt as to what it had to convey. She had seen this word used many times, particularly within fifteenth and sixteenth century texts, to address the viewer (or reader). It was a key word indicating, "Whosoever the reader was, he should consider the instructions herewith."

"When I saw this," Marie continued, "I quickly pulled a pen and paper from my purse, and started working with the text looking for anagrams. I carefully scrutinized the tombstones for typical misspellings or odd spacing. And after a half-hour, I became ecstatic. I had extracted the message, *'Dear Reader, learn from this tomb the exact location of old Bruton's foundations.'* I could barely contain myself, at which point, I ran to find the church vestry."

"Dr. Goodwin, the Minister of Bruton Church, had been ill for quite some time," Marie explained. "So when I initially asked to speak to him, the clerk had refused. But I didn't intend to give up that easily."

Instead, Marie returned and asked the clerk to inform Dr. Goodwin that she had discovered the existence of a vault, buried beneath the graveyard. "Please tell him that the evidence I've found is quite convincing."

Marie went on to explain, that as the clerk hurried off, she was left alone looking around the room nervously – trying to anticipate her course of action. Walking past a bookcase, she impulsively picked up a book on the history of Bruton Parish, and found that Dr. Goodwin had written it himself. After buying a copy, she sat down thumbing through its pages and continued to wait. Minutes later, the clerk reentered and Marie found herself being escorted to the vestry's room.

"When I entered the room, the air was stuffy. The curtains were drawn; it was dark and difficult to see. The only light was a small lamp lit by his bedside, where a small wooden chair was placed for me to sit. As I walked closer, Dr. Goodwin looked pale and sickly. I felt sorry for him as he struggled to wiggle his way up higher onto his pillow to greet me."

As Marie relayed her story, Dr. Goodwin lay there listening to every word. Occasionally he'd shift uncomfortably at the mention of certain things, but other than that, he gave no sign as to how he felt about what she was saying. However, the moment she mentioned going to the Rockefellers, Dr. Goodwin's mood suddenly changed. "After all," Marie said, "they *are* the ones in charge of restoration in this town."

His pale skin, once white, had turned red with rage. He screamed out, "No!" And then began to cough and choke on his words begging her not to go to them. "The Rockefellers have no right to anything that is here at Bruton Parish – anything!" Just then, the clerk broke into the room and quickly ushered Marie out.

"At first I thought this outburst was due to his illness. But I would later learn to regret discounting his warnings."

Later that night, Marie had a chance to look through Dr. Goodwin book about Bruton Church. She had found an important statement that would eventually change the course of events. It revealed that the present Bruton Church was built on the site of an older church, which Marie assumed to be the original Bruton Parish. This hereby confirmed the location of Bruton Vault; since the code had said it would be buried beneath the "original brick foundations." At the time however, she was too excited with her findings, to bother researching records describing the location of two earlier wooden churches at the parish – since they would not have had the brick foundations, as mentioned in the code.

Marie at this point had everything she needed and felt it was certainly enough evidence to convince the Rockefeller Restoration team to dig for the vault. A series of meetings were arranged where the Restoration team, the City Officials and the Church Vestry would meet – over thirty representatives were there. Now it was up to Marie to convince them to approve the dig.

Strange Prophecy

Marie began by exhibiting the code and the tracings she made from the different books she had brought along – all pointing to the existence of the vault, buried right there, beneath their own church.

But what really caught their attention was the *Wither Book;* it seemed to contain a strange prophecy. There, in the drawings were buildings and streets that had not yet existed. The publication of the book preceded their construction by *100 YEARS!* Marie felt that the emblems were architectural blueprints of a future city in the Freemason's New World. This meant that there was a plan in progress – every detail down to the tombstones. Even the poem found in the *Wither Book* seemed to support its mysterious nature:

> *Some Emblems and Poems*
> *Your emblems should, by future generations,*
> *Be placed among the famous constellations,*
> *And after-times, (though mee, this age despise)*
> *Shall think these verses, had been prophecies.*
> *George Wither*

The Rockefeller team was amazed. Taking turns going through the book, a member of the team was suddenly taken aback. He had made a startling discovery – the *Wither Book* revealed an architectural flaw in one of their buildings. An obscure window, that had always been in question, had been incorrectly placed. The accuracy of the drawings and layouts of the streets within the emblems had proven to be astounding. Particularly since the book was written long before the actual streets had been built!

The news of vaults and treasures traveled fast; the entire town was a-buzz. The Rockefeller Restoration team had excitedly chosen the date…and the press, alongside everyone in town, promised to be there.

Bruton Vault

That morning of August in 1938 was an exciting day for Marie – it was the day they would dig for the vault. She had gotten up and dressed by dawn, arriving at the church before anyone else. While standing alone, near the tower reflecting upon the situation at hand, she suddenly noticed that the Nicolson tomb, which she had studied before, was curiously in exact line with the center of the tower, where she stood.

Drawn to the tomb, she knelt at its side and began studying the carved letters running down its face. But for the first time she noticed that the death-date of Nicolson was the same as Sir Francis Bacon's birthday.

"I still don't understand why I hadn't seen this before? I took a quick glance at the men preparing to dig on the other side of the yard and began to panic. As I stared at the numbers, I was overcome by a strange sensation of doubt and trepidation"…she had begun re-processing the steps she used to break down the code.

"That was when I realized that I had never included any *numbers* in the anagrams – numbers could have been used as measurements, describing the location of the vault. But there was no time to check these numbers – the dig was about to begin. I instantly thought about the Vestry's book, which recorded two earlier wooden churches…I began to worry that there may be another brick church built earlier than the existing Bruton Church as well."

When the Vestry and Restorations teams arrived, Marie began to express her doubts as to the location of the first brick church. When they adamantly denied the existence of any other, she questioned them as to the source of their calculations. A tall, slim, arrogant looking man came up to their defense.

"I'm part of the restoration team…I can understand your suspicion; there has always been confusion with the two wooden churches. But I can assure you, we have laid claim to all documents regarding the buildings on these premises and none support the existence of what you refer to, as a second brick church...Simply put, no records have ever surfaced."

"My mind went blank" Marie continued, "there was nothing I could do. After a short speech by the Restoration Team, the floor to the existing church was removed."

Marie stood watching the excavations within a roped off area filled with a small crowd of spectators, officials and newspapermen. Curiously, she noticed that the ground they were digging had already been disturbed. She was too anxious to think that anyone else could have recently dug there before.

At nine feet, the diggers hit brick. But as they dug around it, they found only an arch and disappointment quickly filled the air.

When the vault wasn't found, the Restoration team had lost confidence in her information and withdrew all support. The arch was never investigated and they immediately covered over the entire trench.

Yet Marie would not give up. She knew the vault *had* to be somewhere near. The code, the books, the evidence she found was far too convincing. But in order to reignite the interest of the Vestry, she would now have to find definitive, *physical* proof that the original Bruton Parish was located somewhere else. And the only way she could do this was by locating *official* records that would support her theories – records that they said, didn't exist.

Early the next morning, while it was still dark, she snuck out to the graveyard carrying a long roll of tissue paper and some chalk, moving from one gravesite to the next, making rubbings of each inscription. While perched on one of the tombs completing a rubbing, a young man quickly strolled by on his way to work. Taking one glance at Marie, he screamed and ran off.

"I only realized later, that I had smeared white chalk dust all over my face and arms giving the illusion I was a ghost..."

The Tombstones

Tombstones were quite a clever way to hide information. After all, there were all sorts of numbers on tombstones to give size and direction. Marie knew that any of the tombstones that were encoded would stand out among the others, if properly placed.

As she looked across the graveyard, she noticed that there were five tombstones strategically lined up near the church. Two of them were squared to one another – which she thought could indicate where the tower of a church might be. Then she saw three other **tombstones** strategically spaced apart from the original two – these three were placed as if to indicate the body of a church.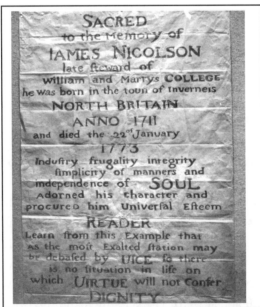

After making rubbings of the distinctly placed tombstones, Marie hurried across the street, spending the day working on ciphers:

These ciphers were then compared with the anagrams from books and tombstone rubbings she had gotten earlier on. She was sure these epitaphs would contain additional encoded messages left behind by "Bacon and his group," the secretive Freemasons:

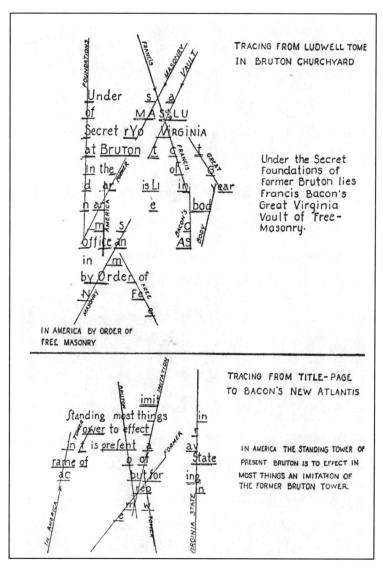

TRACING FROM LUDWELL TOMB IN BRUTON CHURCHYARD

Under the Secret Foundations of Former Bruton lies Francis Bacon's Great Virginia Vault of Free-Masonry.

IN AMERICA BY ORDER OF FREE MASONRY

TRACING FROM TITLE-PAGE TO BACON'S NEW ATLANTIS

IN AMERICA THE STANDING TOWER OF PRESENT BRUTON IS TO EFFECT IN MOST THINGS AN IMITATION OF THE FORMER BRUTON TOWER.

Nevertheless, Marie knew that the tombstones could not be her only proof. Stronger evidence was needed. Remembering Dr.

Godwin's book mentioning other churches built at Bruton Parish, she began by investigating the official records at the church vestry.

"When I returned to the vestry to look at the records – regarding churches that were built on the parish site *before* the present church – the clerk seemed to hesitate and eye me suspiciously. After alerting someone on the phone of my presence, she disappeared into a file room, returning a few minutes later, carrying a large leather-bound book in hand."

Marie continued to explain that she was ushered to a small wooden table, and then left alone to study the book's contents. Excitedly, she opened the book only to find that someone had torn out some of its pages. In fact, all records previous to the erection of present Bruton Church, built in 1715, had been completely torn away.

Since Marie knew she wouldn't get any answers from the clerk, she decided to pay a visit to the old sexton at the church – someone whom she had befriended, and very supportive of her endeavor. Unbeknownst to Marie, he would hold the key to her findings.

When Marie found the old sexton, he was on his hands and knees digging up the weeds growing over a tomb. And after explaining her dilemma, she asked about Dr. Goodwin's book and the two wooden churches. The old sexton explained that Dr. Goodwin had told him about a picture of Bruton Church, he had found while working one evening at William and Mary College. The strange thing was, that this picture looked nothing like the present Bruton Church.

This was all Marie needed. She, and a few college students, who had become supporters interested in her plight, scoured the college library searching for the sketch. It was a week before they finally found a reference in an old Virginia magazine of a sketch, drawn in 1699, by a German traveler named Michel.

He had drawn the sketch when the *original* church would have been standing. And although this sketch had not been titled, it plainly illustrated a brick church – its brick pattern clear and concise – its importance stressed by the mere fact that artist had omitted the two wooden churches nearby:

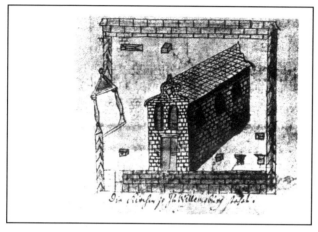

They took the sketch and made inquiries into other maps drawn during the same time. Whereby Marie discovered an old English map, found at the public Research Room of the Restoration. It was the Bland Map, also drawn in 1699, used by The Restoration Team as the basic layout of Williamsburg.

This map had a lengthy legend that included measurements given in "poles" for east and west directions, while attaching the point of measurement to the lower corner scaled the north and south. She also noticed that the legend was credited to Nicolson – reminding her, yet again, of the Nicolson Tomb.

Marie went back to the Restoration team, and asked if the location of the present church had been checked against the Bland map. "Of course" was their response to Marie. Then she asked if they had done a survey to make sure. Condescendingly, they explained, that there had long been a dispute as to where the starting point for the measurements should be taken at William and Mary College. And without a starting point, a survey was not considered. "All this meant to me was that they were actually unsure of the measurements, and if a survey could be done this far into the restoration, they may be somewhat embarrassed of any mistakes it may reveal."

Back to Nicolson's Grave

It was then, that Marie made another important breakthrough. She realized that she had never included the dates or numbers in her anagrams. This was an important piece of the puzzle. The numerals in connection with anagrams, *could* replicate each other, thereby verifying the information encoded. So Marie, along with a few college supporters, went back to the Nicolson inscriptions.

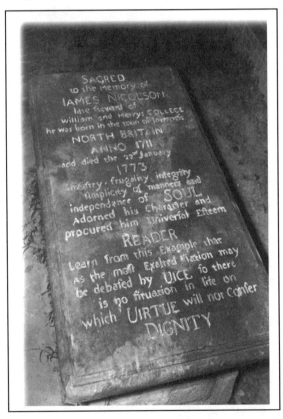

With tracings of Nicolson's tomb and maps spread out on the table, the small group excitedly decoded the numbers to pin the distances down – while Marie, through the use of anagrams, verified the numbers. With this information, they calculated that the present tower center was "1,773" *(date of death)* feet – east of William and Mary College, and the old tower center would be the *(date of birth)* 1711 feet – east of the college:

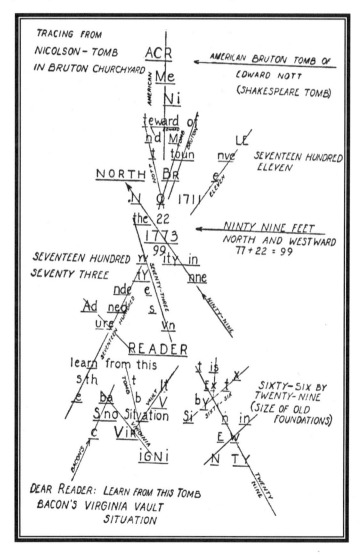

It was this calculation that did away with any ambiguity of the *starting point* – or the point of origin for measurement. After converting the poles into feet, Marie and her committee of supporters came to the conclusion that the older brick church on the Bland Map would be 62 feet west of where the present Bruton Church sat.

The Dig

Although Marie was able to convince the county surveyor to confirm her calculations, all her work was done in vain. When she went back to show the principles of the restoration team all her evidence, they flatly refused to have anything more to do with it. Permission to dig again was flatly denied.

With no support, there was only one thing left to do…Marie, a loyal supporter, and a hired hand, got up early the next morning in 1938 and illegally dug up the specified area within the churchyard in search of the vault. By sun-up, following the instructions and dimensions given on the tombstones, Marie found what she had searched for: *the **original brick church foundation**.* However, before she and the others could dig beneath the foundation and unearth the vault, the church Vestry discovered her. She was ordered to stop, under the threat of arrest. 🕮

The Restoration team was livid – Marie had discovered the location of the original foundations and proven them wrong. Just as she had calculated, the foundation was precisely the size and shape deciphered from the codes. After many meetings with city and church officials, it was tentatively agreed that excavation of the foundation would be resumed. However, the happiness of gaining their support was short-lived. As soon as the final excavation of the foundations was completed, the Vestry decided to delay the actual search for the vault.

"They wanted to wait until the excitement died down and the situation gotten back in-hand. I didn't mind the delay…I actually preferred locating the vault with things less hectic, so I agreed."

"Police guards were stationed at the site," Marie went on, "and the churchyard doors were closed for the first time in years. They told me not to speak to anyone, particularly the press. And consequently, an article appeared in the local paper about the 'newly discovered foundations,' with not one mention of my name or the crucial work I had done. Whenever I confronted them, the vestry responded with a threat to abandon the dig."

Marie's supporters were incensed. Letters in support of her endeavor were sent out. At a public meeting, the head of the Rockefeller Restoration team made the statement, "The finding of old Bruton's foundation is the most unfortunate thing that has ever happened to Williamsburg, and should never have been permitted."

While weeks of meetings went by, Marie focused on contacting Mr. Lundberg of Ontario, Canada, who owned a firm that could conduct an **"equipotential survey"** of the original Bruton foundation. This was a study requiring scientific instruments that could detect underground anomalies – particularly since the anagrams revealed that the contents of the vault had been placed in copper cylinders.

Marie convinced Mr. Lundberg to send his engineer, Mark Malamphy who donated his time to run the tests. And after the report was done, Malamphy went before the Vestry and Restoration team to explain his findings – presenting them with graphical maps. First he explained the methods used in his impartial tests:

An alternating current is introduced into the ground by means of two bare conductors, grounded at several points and arranged parallel to each other on opposite sides of the area to be investigated. Two metallic probes are connected with the amplifiers and telephones, and are employed in tracing out an equipotential surface of the ground. When the electric current is introduced into the earth by means of two parallel linear electrodes, grounded at numerous points, the current will flow from one electrode to the other along essentially straight lines. However if a foreign body of electrical characteristics different from the surrounding medium is to be found in the area under consideration, the pass of the current line will be distorted and the determined points will connect to a curvature.

The result of this engineer's report read: "At a depth of from sixteen to twenty feet, about ten feet square, centered exactly where the 1711 line east of William and Mary College crosses the old foundations lies a body partially filled and much larger than an ordinary tomb."

But since this sort of survey had never been used in this manner before, it lacked, they said, "credibility." While members of the Vestry were in favor of excavations, members of the Restoration began to insinuate that Malamphy had "made the spot coincide with Marie's findings." Then finally, after a few days, and a great deal of deliberation, the city officials demanded that the excavations be resumed, yet again.

The next morning, they had dug to a depth of nearly five feet with Restoration archeologists sneering with remarks like, "This time when we don't find anything, you can't say someone's dug here before…this ground's never been disturbed, unless God Almighty did it himself."

As they dug deeper, a casket was found, but they weren't allowed to remove any of the dirt around it unless it had fallen off. The digging continued and although more difficult, there was still no change in the composition of the ground.

The following day the inexplicable happened. At a depth of nine feet, the excavations were ordered to stop and the next day the trench was covered up. When Malamphy requested that at least a cross trench be dug, the committee refused. The reason was they didn't want to disturb the casket that was found, nor the Graham tomb nearby. And though Malamphy's findings indicated an anomaly, they used the excuse that it was probably caused by a "high point in a bed of marl." Even though true marl was generally not found above fifty feet – they had dug only nine…and studied the earth no further.

The church wanted to close the subject and the Rockefellers accused Marie of interfering with their work.

"When they covered it up, I cried."

Edgar Cayce, the renowned psychic, and the townspeople, came down in the midst of it all to lend their support. But the digging was never to be resumed.

"Did you ever go back?" I asked.

"No."

I still had so many questions. Could the tomb have been moved? Fred had told me about underground tunnels or passageways that coursed beneath Bruton Parish and its surrounding area. Could someone have entered the vault from underground, without having to disturb the soil? Someone would have had plenty of time to move the vault between the day Marie dug up the foundations and the days that it took the restoration committee and City Council to finally decide to resume the digging, then finally cover it up.

And what of the uncanny accuracy of the tombstones…Nicolson's tomb in particular? Was there actually a body buried beneath, or was this tomb placed as a guidepost for future generations to find.

The David Bray tomb proved to be as much a mystery as the others. Its pyramidal form held an uncanny resemblance to the one in the Wither Book. It had been said that during the Civil War, the monument was demolished then rebuilt as the current one. Could the *original* **Bray tomb** have been identical to the emblem in the Wither Book…with its symbol of the astrological sign of Taurus (representing treasure) resting atop? And when Marie had asked the diggers to dig a trench around the tomb, they found its base (lying beneath the surface) to be nine foot square and three feet deep; constructed with the same bricks as the foundations and topped by a stone-plate – far overbuilt for a tomb that size.

The placement of the Bray tomb is just as interesting; it rests within the foundations, where the alter of the original church would have been. And though these tombs could not have been placed there until after the first church was torn down ("except the brick"), the dates of their deaths were well before the present church was built. Marie had said that the "new Church was finished about December 1715, and on November 16th, 1716 an order was made by the Vestry that the Church Warden dispose of all the material belonging to the Old Church, except the brick. In 1717 the new Church was shingled."

When Marie had asked that the Bray tomb be investigated, the Vestry said that the Bray family would have to be consulted. She was told that the property where the tomb rested, along with its immediate surrounding area, was the only land outside the Vestry's jurisdiction. When one of the Vestry members stopped to ask if this could be where the treasure was buried, she said no, and that it would need to be ten foot square, buried much deeper. Could there have been a miscalculation?

The Bray tomb was the only tomb in the graveyard with a Latin inscription; Guil Bray is a signature that lies beneath the Latin inscription on the front page within the Wither Book.

And when I spoke to Fred Cole again, his story still continued to fascinate me. Fred had sent for a **map** of Williamsburg and made a strange discovery: the legend of the map appeared to designate Bruton Church as a *military reservation.* How could church property be designated a military reservation?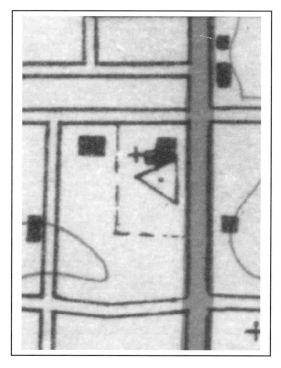

But at least this explained why the Rockefellers, who were refurbishing Williamsburg at the time, were not allowed to purchase this property.

Fred had also found a strange notation in a book by John Tyler, a statement that a Cornel Page donated the Bruton Parish property. In the signing, it reads: "Till time immemorial." This was known as a Masonic phrase, again, linking Sir Francis Bacon to his involvement with the vault – as stated in the Wither's code.

Years later, an independent group who had read Marie's works on Bruton Vault brought in special equipment to search for copper metal in that area of the grounds, but nothing was ever found. However, a letter from a man who worked on that second survey added to the mystery. He informed her that the search was incomplete. They felt that they should have checked the other end of the original foundation, in the event the map was reversed. In 1991, another group headed by Marsha Middleton had unsuccessfully tried to dig it up as well. And though Marie somehow felt that the vault had been moved, others still say that the mystery remains.

Marie's Bruton experience no doubt, had implications on a grand scale. She had sat with all of us relating her story and given me volumes of writings and her recordings. However, though my imagination was triggered, I was still faced with the task of how this story fit into the body of her work? What relation did it have to the Arcanum she had begun to reveal? Furthermore, where did she begin?

Path of Discovery

When Marie returned home, she had thrown herself solely into her research. Finding the foundations was enough to convince her that a greater plan was being revealed.

She studied the emblems in the *Wither Book* and found many of them depicted members of the Bacon group, relating their "fates, labors and difficulties." And there were emblems and poems that represented Queen Elizabeth, Shakespeare, Robert Deveraux, and others.

But her most important revelation was her discovery of Bacon's works along with its codes. Through her search she had found that Bacon had discovered the Arcanum himself...the mysterious origins and causes of the universe within nature – and its Divine Plan through which man would come to this understanding, or enlightenment. She further explained, that Bacon and his group had been chosen to preserve these hidden teachings within an encoded pattern, to be buried within all forms of text, art and architecture. This would thereby sustain and perpetuate its message (hiding it from the profane), making it available for the purpose of igniting the minds of ALL free men, not merely the learned and religious hierarchy.

Within the codes she found that Bacon and his group petitioned other contemporaries to infuse these fundamental ideas, patterns and symbols into the art and literature of *their* time, and with further scrutiny found that Bacon's influence had expanded to the very original government charters upon which our own nation was founded.

After finding there was far more to Bacon's involvement than she had anticipated, she threw herself into the study of Bacon and his contemporaries.

With this work her mind became sharpened and conditioned into seeing through the art, symbols, and anagrams buried within the texts that were laid before her. Each day was met with a new revelation. And as her intensity towards the understanding of the work heightened, something deep, strange, and powerful began to move within her. The pattern, the original blueprint for her existence, was ignited – the Life and intelligence of God, soared through her veins.

Something began to take over, *something that wanted her to see.* Thus the visions began – the diagrams she drew became the only language through which she could interpret the things she saw…she had entered Bacon's sphere, penetrating the mysteries: The invisible worlds of origins and causes lay stretched before her. Here is where she lived, died, and was born again to dream the dreams of the One.

"It was within this timelessness," she explained, *"all was the One."* She could see the minutest details within the essence of time and matter, overlaying particles within space and the substance of the mind. She saw the origins of gravity and the inception of a moving glow of energy as physical light.

When Marie returned to her writings, she did her best to write them down. Her strength was that she believed in this Divine Plan or Order within the universe – for it could never have been revealed to a vessel of one who was unsure.

It was these revelations that lead Marie to what would be *her* Life's Assignment – what I came to refer to as the "Arcana Arcanum" (Mystery of Mysteries). And through her work I too would search and dig through the disheveled mountains of notes, tapes, books, and manuscripts, to discover…that it was her work with the Arcanum, and its teachings that was the *real treasure.* The doctrine taught within her visions themselves, *was* what lay hidden within the darkened tomb, buried in the graveyard of Bruton Church. This treasure was not of the physical world, objects left to deteriorate within the Earth's womb. It was a

Divine Idea brought to light, reemerged for the awakening of man's Soul.

Marie said that, *woman was made to break the secrets wide open...* and that is what she did.

❖

The Divine Plan Revealed

I soon learned that most of the people who came through Marie's life were particularly interested in the mystery of Bruton Vault. These visitors seemed to be captivated with its cryptic nature, marveling at the possibilities it would unveil for mankind. And though, I too, found her story of Bruton Vault intriguing, I knew it was only the tip of what was yet to unfold – a different kind of treasure…*the profound cosmogony that lie buried beneath it all.*

Some said her cosmological writings were obscure and burdensome as though channeled and haphazardly written down. Others said it was repetitive lacking order in thought. And there were times that even I wondered, while looking through her work, if it were either genius or true madness. It would take years to find the answer, years to see beyond her strange use of words, into the essence of its invisible order. And after dissecting the work, using keywords to organize the materials, I realized why Marie had written in this manner. The Arcanum was all there, for Marie could intuitively see – was aware of – *all dimensions at once.* However, her three-dimensional faculties limited her ability to interpret these visions in a linear order. Her mind seemed to be altered, moving from one dimension to another, filtering the information and only able to master one idea at a time.

It was like seeing hundreds of glittering images all at once – like moving pictures falling through the air. The viewer, over-inundated by the images before them, and handicapped or limited by his faculties, must absorb as much as they can of this overall view; but they can only focus on one image at a time – regardless of its order. Hence Marie's writings reflected her ability to isolate an idea being transmitted from this immense collage of cosmic panorama.

Because of the nature of what was in hand, I found that the only way to extract the essence of her writings was to first break

79

everything down. Her language and use of specific words would need to be understood. To accomplish this, I would begin by retracing her *path of discovery...to read everything that she had read – and had written.* I needed to find the intent behind her work. And since Bacon played such an intricate role in her initial research, I thought I should start there too.

Bacon's Plan

Who was this Sir Francis Bacon? I knew very little about him except that he was born in 1561 and was considered to have resurrected and energized the fraternal order of the Freemasons.[8] Other than that, his past and my own spiritual path had really never crossed.

When I asked Marie who Bacon was, she went on to reveal an esoteric side to his life completely different than the historical writings I had begun to research.

Marie contended: At a very early age, Bacon had been contacted, and schooled by a group of highly, spiritually evolved individuals referred to as the *Ascended Masters*. *The Ascended Masters*, sometimes called the *White Brotherhood*, were in charge of an elite Masonic Group to which, in their care, was left the responsibility of helping to initiate the progressive stages that will move mankind towards their enlightenment.

Sir Francis Bacon was chosen because he held the keys to the secret knowledge of all ages – buried within the memories of his Soul. He had absorbed this great understanding during what Marie referred to as, his incarnation* while *Peter of the Apostles*.

Bacon as Peter, along with the other Apostles, had experienced the Pentecost Miracle – where the Holy Spirit had

---

[8] Secret fraternal society.
* The concept of reincarnation is linked to DNA Studies. Science is helping to redefine how information is transferred in the human being.

come down and enlightened their minds and Souls to the mysteries of all life. Through enlightenment, they had been given access to *Apostolic* documenting of the past, present, and future of earth history. The revelation of these mysteries, from within, was to become part of their Soul's memories. Hence, the miracle of this deeper understanding of life would stay with them throughout all subsequent incarnations – thereby becoming part of intelligence within the code of their DNA.

This was how Bacon was able to re-discover the meaning of the *Lost Word,* because the memories lay within his Soul. Marie believed that the *Lost Word,* if truly understood, would not only reveal the *Divine Plan* – the steps and stages of creation and how man would achieve immortality – but the true understanding of God itself, ultimately leading an individual to a *self-governing* state.

Within this self-governing state, the initiate is not only aware of one's responsibility for past deeds, but he is consciously developing a process of "wakefulness"…a practice of being mentally and spiritually present within the moment – or simply "being." This process, of self-governing would eventually evolve beyond self-observation…becoming Soul-observation. This not only purifies, causing the transformation of the initiate, but would also bring one to a **sustainable, purely aware state** with dominion over nature itself; for within this state of awareness, one taps into a Universal mind that is intrinsic to all that exists.

Bacon had concealed the knowledge of this process in the early Masonic works of the Freemasons, just as the ancients had hidden their great knowledge within the design of the pyramids. Marie believed that the pyramid's form, its dimensions, shape and size, was a symbol or code, which if understood, would reveal their mysteries.

The pyramidal form itself was used as a physical model or monument, symbolizing the ancients' deeper understanding of what Marie called, "laws and ways of the evolution of form, being provoked by life involution." In other words, form evolved so that it could sustain the varying degrees of life intelligence evolving and incarnating within these forms: *the higher the intelligence, the more evolved the form.*

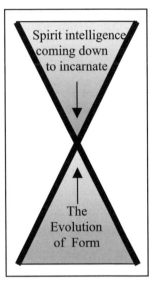

Marie also discovered that Bacon's model revealed that the process through which a Human-author takes an idea and draws his thoughts on paper as written text, could be compared to the Divine Author, God, taking its ideas and manifesting them as the text of *nature...Nature is God's text.* For example, where a human author uses a pen and blank paper, the Divine Author uses matter and space (paper) to write or create nature. Nature is God's ideas made manifest. (See Appendix One.)

Marie explained that Bacon had found the process in which a human author's idea expressed in writing (the alphabet, evolving to word, then sentence), could be used to symbolize the stages and steps taken by matter evolving within Kingdoms of Nature – i.e. the alphabet symbolized the mineral kingdom; word was symbolic of the vegetable kingdom, etc.

She believed that Bacon then developed a code based on this understanding through which he could hide the information, burying it for centuries within his writings. She functioned on the premise that if one were to understand Bacon's "coordinated system of codes" one would find the secret of organic life and the mystery of man's make-up.* It would be like following Ariadne's thread – a labyrinth that leads us through nature's mysteries – and at the center we find the very *Life Principle* that motivates nature to proceed.

> *As single letters in due sequence set,*
> *Make up these words, and words to phrases moulded,*
> *Give Love's fond tongue to that dull alphabet*
> *That sealed them as a cypher trice enfolded;*
> *So are the shapes of Nature's outward show,*
> *The scattered characts we aright must fit,*
> *A message hid within a criss-cross row,*
> *Till we by searching find the key to it...*
> *(Sonnets of G.S.O) (P.246)*

Bacon would call this code his "invention"-- an invention that carried the hidden life of the *Soul's Intelligence.* Marie said the pattern of this code could be seen within anyone's writings - created unconsciously. And if we understood this universal code, no matter what the cover-text (or *outward show*) would read, we could extract the hidden text...the true message of what the person was really thinking as they wrote.

That evening, when I got home, I dug into my library looking for anything I could find on Sir Francis Bacon. As I read, something caught my eye: *The Divine Plan.* This phrase kept repeating itself throughout all of the articles. Bacon felt that by concealing the mysteries of Life, it would stimulate man to seek more diligently for God's Word, His Divine Plan. Could this be what Marie had discovered – a glimpse of Bacon's Divine Plan revealed? Was the Divine Plan, the same as the Divine

---

* This process would reveal the quantity and quality of energy and other components that go into the makeup of matter.

"Word"...Word being the *idea* or *sound* of creation made manifest? Could the thousands of pages of work that we were pulling together be the result of her initial study of Bacon's plan or the discovery of "God's Divine Plan" at work...the *Divine Return to Oneness,* its stages and steps broken down and recorded as it is in the process of living?

Bacon had said that nature would not give up its secrets to man so easily. Was he asking it for himself, or was he warning us, that we must become more responsible before the infinite power of nature and life reveal itself? Perhaps he was trying to tell us that the process of finding the answers to unraveling the secrets of nature was the very same process to purification or enlightenment of man. This process is likened to the Alchemist, whose *search* for the Opus Magnum[9] is the very preparation to receive it.

In the book *Bacon's Masonry*, it is said that few Masons knew the true meaning of the Divine Plan. Yet, if one looks at history and the individuals who have been Masons, including many U.S. presidents and world leaders, we see the enormous power and influence the Masons have had over the centuries as political and financial leaders around the world.

Bacon's Unified Theory

Marie spoke of Bacon being known as the *regenerator of Freemasonry.* He used the Masonic order as a vehicle to carry the principles of fellowship into the busy lives of businessmen and tradesmen, who would then become the backbone of all nations. And in the field of religion, he kept the torch of true universal knowledge alive during the dark night of the Middle Ages.

Marie had discovered that his true mission was to create the foundation upon which the sectarianism of diverse religions might give rise to a *Unified Theory of World Spirituality* – a

---

[9] The Divine work of creation.

prophecy of the now evolving global community. Though apparently based on key components within Christianity, it would be a belief system that represents all ideologies, one that could help humanity reach a deeper level of thinking, an understanding of life that can only be found within the *essence* of things at its core. It was a process of unification, the development of a viewpoint of Oneness, pure awareness, which I call *God Point*...seeing from God's point of view.

Through *God Point*, we see unification begin, our differences start to melt away; the images or lines of separation that divide a form are dissolved; the veil of Maya, illusion is lifted, thus allowing a *pattern* to emerge within existence. This pattern is underlying the makeup of both physical and non-physical form-worlds. By identifying this pattern it not only reveals Life essences on a chemical level, but it ignites or awakens a process within us, that transforms the way we think – moving us towards a pure state of awareness. Here we begin to experience, our own immersion into a sea of living intelligence, which can only love...simply that. It moves in a divine order, and this *pattern, lines of Life and light,* of which we are a fraction – contains and sustains all that exists.

With the development of God Point, through which we craft the images of our existence, we are lead to the further development of the brain and organs. They are our antennas. And only by perfecting our physical body, in a natural balance with Spirit, mind, and Soul, can the intensity of a higher level of consciousness be absorbed and sustained.

Within these higher stages of consciousness, man could then expand into the realm of pure awareness, whereby his spiritmind and natural mind are aligned with the patterning of his Soulmind. As this alignment is reached, a *second heat is struck.* He sees his destiny and a vision of his own potential of perfection. He is energized, given the capacity to make transition to his next incarnation, or finally consumed by the vessel of Oneness.

Marie believed that Bacon, being a deeply religious man with a broad sense of the human condition, knew that a Unified theory of Spirituality would not be easy to bring about. He would have to devise a plan for the preparation and dissemination of this Divine Knowledge or Ideology. And there were so many factors to consider. Since human development was dependent upon its intelligence factor and level of spiritual understanding, its dissemination had to be carefully orchestrated.

First, he needed the tools to carry this information, tools that could help in *quickening* the minds of men, *re-conditioning* their ways of thinking, becoming aware of the *deeper mysteries of life*. Who better to discover the foundations of these tools than the "Father of Modern Science," himself, Sir Francis Bacon?

I have been induced to think that if there were a Beam
Of Knowledge derived from God, upon any Man In these
Modern Times, it was upon him.
　　　Dr. W. Rawley, 1670
　　　(in reference to Sir Francis Bacon)

Bacon was the originator of the Inductive Method of Reasoning. This method led to our present-day industrialism. As industrialism gave birth to the new sciences and technologies, i.e. electricity, radio, television, film, computers, etc., one could then use these new tools to anticipate the learning needs of the collective – and thereby release the appropriate *scientific* information and inventions that would help disseminate specific information at the proper time.

Bacon was not only aware of the importance of multi-sensory learning, but intuitively knew that the learning process of future man, with his higher developed consciousness and thought process, would require new tools through which he could be educated.

The Mind & Technology

Today, we witness some of the effects and influences that these tools have on man through television and film. We live in an audio-visual world that *elicits both the seeing and the hearing of the natural mind[10] at the same time.* This thereby allows the scene (on the screen) to be experienced from within, mesmerizing us – suspending our disbelief. While the *natural mind* is kept busy with deciphering the mechanical bits of information it sees and hears on the screen (*surface* material), there is nothing blocking the Truth or the true intent of the message. Depending on if the message is positive or negative, it will either flow straight through to the Soul or for the building of the ego or self!

In the case of a positive message: with nothing blocking the Soul, the learning process itself is *quickened*...the incoming information, now being directly experienced by the Soul, is turned into subtle essences that are absorbed directly into the Soul-mind...bypassing the natural mind (with its fears and limitations) that normally stop the information from getting through to the Soul. This newly influenced Soul may then parentally transmit, through their *DNA,* these hopefully positive messages into the future souls of their offspring. This is why Marie believes that Hollywood could be the next Holy-land. The visual industry has a great deal of power over our Natural Minds, and in their own way can inhibit or precipitate the Soul's growth and the advancement of humankind.

In the case of a negative message: the learning process is quickened and instead of the incoming information being experienced through the Soulmind, it is directly experienced by the spiritmind...used by the ego. Here the information empowers the ego, releasing fears and limitations that are incorporated into the

---

[10] Natural mind is connected to the brain and bound to the physical form. (See: Spiritmind; Soulmind)

Spiritself (spirit + self/ego) of the individual, thereby enhancing its need for control.

In Bacon's *New Atlantis* he calls our world "the New Atlantis, which you will call America." I would hope that we New Atlanteans will use our power and influence to the betterment and service of mankind!

In 1942 Marie had discovered that the following poster had been distributed to all the elementary schools in the country. She identified Bacon shown as a ghost (see hat) orchestrating the building of America. The paper Bacon is holding, added to its mystery:

Red Cross Poster

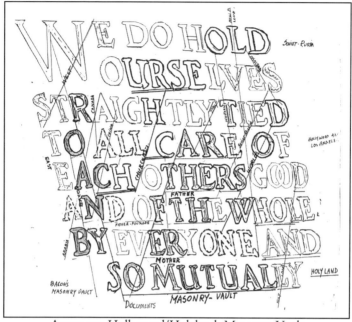

Anagrams: Hollywood/Holyland, Masonry, Vault
(Scroll held within Bacon's hands)

Since Bacon had envisioned a world of scientific discoveries that could carry this knowledge, he would also need a plan, a way to implement these tools within *all* departments of human endeavor – accessible to all and not just a few. This would mean that enlightened, or *eligible* men and women connected to the plan, both knowingly and unknowingly, had to be placed in influential and strategic positions throughout the world (i.e. governmental or corporate positions) to create the way that would propel the dissemination of the message.

Bacon also needed a *great span of time.* This meant that secrecy and concealment was necessary so that these principles of brotherhood would be permitted to grow, slowly and *unnoticed*, into the *fabric* of the nations that were to later consciously understand them.

And because a span of time was needed, there had to be a method to preserve the Divine Writings. Therefore, this information would be hidden within various countries and nations buried within vaults, hidden within encoded writings. There also had to be a way of preserving historical records and objects that verify and outline the execution of Bacon's plan. To prepare for all of this, economic and political reforms were undertaken that would later act as its confirmation (i.e. the Reformation, French Revolution, abolishment of slavery, World War I, to name a few).

Finally, once the tools, specific people and organization within a span of time is in place, Bacon needed a *New Race*, or new nation of men, destined to be the nucleus of the future Utopia of the Earth. This nation would be representational of ALL nations under God, so that its ideas could be perpetuated throughout the DNA of ALL NATIONALITIES of mankind. This new nation was America, as Bacon referred to as the New Atlantis. This America would represent *all* nationalities and religions...*living in peace*. Its peoples would need to be free, free to have the *opportunity* to search for truth. From here, a new race would be born and grow with a vision of a world where the concept of nationalism would take on a new meaning. If we anagram, reconstructing all the letters in the word America, we can build the new words, "I Am race."

The Second Coming

This *new race* had to be a representation of the entire collective because it would be from these Souls that a certain number of the population or "lawfully required" would emerge representing the collective...at the Second Coming. This correlates with the First Coming, where Christ became the *one* man who was the *lawfully required* by God to represent the entire collective of *His* time.

This certain number of the collective, thought to be the 144,000, was not to be the actual number of people who would become enlightened leaving the rest of us doomed – the amount was symbolic of the number of Souls required to achieve a state of awareness and understanding of God, so that the rest could make the shift in consciousness. This shift would be somewhat likened to the "100th monkey effect"* or *morphic resonance (formative causation)* – when "?" amount becomes enlightened, the entire collective makes an automatic shift to the next state of consciousness. This shift directs us toward the ultimate goal within the Divine Plan, *redemption* or recreation of our being, and restoration...to return to our Source (God beyond God our creator) and reabsorbed into its Being.

Marie felt that Bacon had written his Divine Plan with the intention of a *true One-World and Family Enlightened Order.* However the problem was, that it is man's nature to absorb the power and resources for his "self." Marie explained that this became apparent when the inner group (Bacon and his colleagues) elected to carry out the plan, began to split into two factions: the "White Forces," who worked to develop the plan for a "One World *Spirituality*," and the "Dark Forces," consumed by greed, and intent on distorting the vision, renaming it the "One World Order. These Dark Forces became leaders that had forgotten the true reason for their order. This outer Fraternity, originally chosen for selective schooling for adequate leadership in economic-political fields, had chained themselves to the lower desires of man.

New Order of the Ages

I sat down one evening after visiting Marie, and began to think about the process that had been outlined in Bacon's Plan. I

---

* An experiment done in the 50's where one monkey on an island is taught to wash a particular fruit, and once all the monkeys on the island are doing the same, the monkeys on a completely separate island (that hadn't been taught) start to follow the same.

was looking for signs within our day that correlated with the initial steps Bacon had taken. I first looked for tools, which would unite the collective – tools whose language and fundamental use would unify us as a whole. I found one as an example, right away – the computer and the Internet.

We all know that the global influence of computers and the internet are forcing ever-greater numbers of people to return to school, to become educated, so as to have access to knowledge. With this knowledge comes a greater understanding of not only ourselves, but also our responsibility to the world around us. This leads us to become *self-governing* – to *consciously* take responsibility of our own part in the Divine Plan for humanity. This is about a One World or Unified Theory of Spirituality that would move us towards our next stage of development…**not a one-world order of government.**

The computer not only affects our minds, but when used properly, it can also connect us to nature. It was then, that I was posed the question: What is at the heart of the computer? "The crystal!" Nature and the mechanics of intelligence welded into one. I could see the spirit of nature with a personality of its own. My computer, had at *its* heart, a living intelligence, which can be tapped into because it is the same intelligence at the core of our being.

Then I started to break down Bacon's plan. I looked at the way in which these tools would be governed. The Internet, because of its global nature, forces us to find a new way of governing – one in which all aspects of our society, financially, politically, and moralistically would have to be taken into consideration. And since it is a tool that helps to teach us to *self-govern*, then naturally, it would have to be ruled by the people themselves – *vox populi*, the voice of the people.

Today, as we build humanity's future global infrastructure, we have the freedom and ability to choose integrity and honesty in its development. And if we choose to focus on the "lower desires of man," fate will inevitably step in to redesign it to meet *its* original cause…hopefully without lending itself to war.

Only a TRUE One-World and Family ENLIGHTENED Order will unify all nations, setting up newly developed global standards, which will not allow the focusing of power in *one* place. This will also require, thus lead, to a One-World and Family currency. A unified currency would require global policies and laws, taking the highest morals and standards most universally accepted. These universal policies and laws would eventually lead to a *universal understanding* that would embrace the most universally accepted moral standards from the essence of the various religions and ideologies. The essence of this *universal understanding* would then lead to a One-World and Family Age of Enlightenment…even if it takes another 2,000 years! In Bacon's plan, time is irrelevant…there will always be others to carry on. World enlightenment will come!

On our original dollar bill is inscribed: "NOVUS ORDO SECLORUM," *or THE NEW ORDER OF THE AGES!* Here we see that "of the Ages," enlists Time: a new One World Spirituality is to begin and grow in time. At the base of the pyramid is inscribed MDCCLXXVI or 1776, the birth date of this nation. From this base ascend thirteen secretive Masonically supervised layers of brick, ascending toward the all-seeing eye. The eye signifies the anticipated rebirth and reborn waking of enlightenment. In terms of time, thirteen decades added to 1776, brings us to the turn of the century. This is when Masonic supervision over *trial and error* democracy ceased and the growing New World representation of the collective would have to survive and grow on its own!

Again, observing our emblem in terms of time, approximately seven to eight more layers of "invisible brick," or seven to eight more decades could be added for the completion of the pyramid structure, which brings us to our current time. This period was what Marie called, the Second Coming - the *Second Coming of Love Truth and the Light of Truth to mankind*. In the First Coming, Jesus had brought the warmth-aspect of "Love" to warm us, for man was growing cold with reason. But the Second Coming will "ignite" or "light up" the minds of men, to the understanding of God...revealing the truth of man's origin, purpose, and destiny.

Once the "lawfully required" has been awakened, the next step is the quickening, where Christ consciousness will herald in "Christ Awareness."

Initially, Marie had explained Bacon needed help to carry out this plan. And set out to win the greatest minds of the British Empire and the European continent for co-workers in this stupendous task (33 in all). Because they had gathered for the valiant purpose of "shaking a lance at ignorance," they chose for their symbol, **Pallas Athena.** Their group name was termed the "Spear Shakers." They believed that education would lead to the rational maturity of the human race, thus leading to economic security. Security in turn, provides leisure for the pursuit of learning and the eventual enlightenment on a collective scale. Marie encapsulated her ideas in these words:

Re-education for living,
in place of regimentation for dying.

❖

Marie told of a time when she was struggling with the profound loneliness of her work on the Cosmogony – she had become consumed and isolated.

One day the doorbell rang, but no one was there. A mysterious package, addressed to her, had been left at the foot of the landing. Upon examining the package, the shipping stamp read, "Buenos Aires," with no return address. Someone had anonymously sent her an original **Latin manuscript** written in 1512 A.D. Upon opening it, she noticed a mysterious tracing lying over the cover page. And on the tracing, Marie was surprised to find the letters of her name anagrammatically spelled out before her (see illustration):

Latin Manuscript with the anagram "Maria Bauer"

Marie showed us the book. She said that the illustration was of "Love Truth coming to earth," a figure symbolizing that the Second Coming would descend through the feminine aspect of our being – the Soul. The pregnant woman on the left represents world Christianity. In her right hand she bears the cross of Christ, representing Jesus' rescue of time; and in her left is the tablet of Moses representing the Old and New Testament.

Marie began to compare the symbols in the illustration, to her own life. On the top left kneels a pregnant woman who gives birth to all that is below her. In the lower left corner lie four books, three are unsealed and one stands unread – there is a coincidence: Marie had written four books. And her fourth book remains unprinted, unread, lying within her computer, incomplete. On the bottom right of the illustration lay two measuring sticks marked by roman numerals – Marie interpreted these as mirroring her theory of the *Generation of Number*, the stages and steps to Creation.

As Marie described each detail of the illustration, the impact of her interpretation of the symbolism was astounding. She had perfected the ability to read through things – a technique that would enable her to realize the deeper meaning and significance of the words and symbols that lay before her. She could enter worlds where the ordinary mind rarely interjected itself – filtering through layers of meanings until all that was left was its essence. She was able to let go of the self's consciousness – moving into a state of awareness that would lift the veil of secrecy that hung between the visible and invisible worlds.

❖

Moving Onward

The first part of the job was finished. The filing, cleaning, and organizing were done. *Unknowingly,* our small core group had taken our first and most important step on the path - we had given ourselves in service to one another. We did this both mentally and physically, figuring out a *way* to help Marie organize her works, and sacrificing our time and physical energy as well. By going through the action, we built the intensity that was necessary to get us to the next step in our own initiation into the work. She did not demand this of us, nor was it a prerequisite for gaining access to her teachings. She gave freely of her time and watched as we gave freely of ourselves.

> Love is not love unless it is *alive – in action.*
> For only by going through the action of Love itself,
> can we build the *intensity,* the crucible that carries the heat
> of Love's Divine fire that exalts the evolution of our Being.

Part III

The
Mystery Revealed

Part III

The Mystery Revealed

A few of us had already begun gathering around Marie each day to listen to her lecture on both Bruton Vault and her cosmological vision, the Arcanum (The Mysteries). It started off with a small cadre, sitting around the glass octagon table with our tea and pastries in hand. And sometimes an occasional scientist, scholar or friend of Marie's from some far off land, would join us for the evening.

The room was so peaceful. We'd all sit chatting about the deeper mysteries of life…it was as though the world had been suspended in time. We never knew what subject she was to speak on, and it didn't matter. Just sitting there listening, whether or not we comprehended her abstract theories, gave us a sense of peace – a feeling that we were somehow connected to a greater knowledge.

Whenever Marie described the people she'd met and the places she'd been, the past would come alive. We grew excited at her mention of the graveyard at Bruton Parish, fantasizing about going to Williamsburg to dig up the vault.

Whenever she spoke of her Cosmogony, we sat completely mesmerized. She'd mention things like *eternal* and *eternity-time,* then immediately change the subject to, *how life enters matter.* Marie would skillfully intertwine science, religion, philosophy, and myth. And with just the bits and pieces that she'd shared with us, I could already feel my life, and whole way of thinking about God, slowly transform.

Yet after she spoke, the information was so vast and abstract that it made it difficult to retain. So I utilized available technology (tape recorder, video camera, and computer) to maximize my time with her. In response to our frustration of being unable to grasp these universal concepts, or if we wore a puzzled look, she'd repeat:

Patience...
Let hang on what may.
It takes time for the natural mind
to be conditioned into the understanding
these new dimensional thoughts.

❖

Mystery of the Number Four

One day, as the morning hour chimed in at ten, the mystery was finally revealed. Marie entered the room; the beads on her long dangling earrings were the only sound you could hear. As she seated herself she whispered of the *Mystery of the Number Four* and how the search for the Holy Grail would reveal the mystery of our Souls.

I thought to myself, "What *is* the Mystery of the Number Four?"…Then in that moment, a strangely familiar shift of energy hit the room. I braced myself, focused in on her illuminating words then slowly drifted into a place where I'd longed to be – the journey resumed…she was taking us through what I began to refer to as *The Arcanum*. I humbly offer this interpretation:

*Long before the Big Bang and Creation, even before time itself…there existed only One – for the One-ness had not yet become All-ness or All-encompassing as yet, because there was nothing else but **Itself.***

This Oneness was an Absolute Causal[11] Principle,
*a true one-God concept, **fourfold** in its nature –*
(having four aspects to its being).
These Four Aspects filled all of space.
And all else thereafter, above and below,
*Was made, contained, and sustained by these **Four.***

***Three** of the four aspects were Its Spiritself (spirit + self),*
***masculine and creative** by nature.*
These three electric aspects lay dormant in an unconscious state.[12]

---

[11] Causal: That from which all else comes forth.
[12] We see this process within the human form, where the fetus is first feminine, while its masculine aspects lie dormant in a potential state.

*But the **fourth** aspect was **feminine**, and a **purely selfless**[13], virgin state of being – without self – only a pure, selfless, magnetic **Love** filling all that was.*

*This Love has an intelligence, we call awareness – making it a purely, self-less, **Love Aware Intelligence**.*

And though its three creative aspects lay dormant and unconscious in this darkness... This Love Intelligences is still eternally aware of its own state of being.

And what was this Awareness Intelligence doing? *Dreaming...*

Dreaming involution and evolution throughout all of space. It could see all of Its creation and creatures to come... and all that would return to the Source as one...for these were God's Love and Life Dreams – where this One God could experience the joy of giving Its Love...and in the giving of Its Life.

But these are just dreams...

*The One is a purely selfless state...It needs to give. Its nature is to give, to share Itself...with anyone, anything **outside** of Itself...*

...But to what?

Nothing else exists, but itself!

The manifestation process begins...

---

[13] Selfless: No self (ego)...a pure love awareness; limitless...(it is the self that limits us.)

So, it yearns…it yearns to make Its dreams a reality - for It is aware that it is a purely selfless state…It MUST give, Its nature is to give, to share…with anyone, anything outside itself…Yet nothing else exists but itself.

This yearning to give to anything outside of itself, becomes an intense Self-less desire – magnetic – taking and drawing unto Itself.

A self-less desire that consumes with its own flames of Love…burning, heating, and then…engulfing Its own being…

This was the cause of the *Big Bang*…it's what drew the mass (heat) together…God's yearning, God's Self-less & intense desire to share Its Love:

*And through love the One God perpetually breathes in Its own four aspects of Its being, inhaling Its four ingredients – transforming and recreating them – until the heat becomes so intense – that Its selfless desire to share its Love, grows beyond what can be endured – and in that moment, the magnetic **essence of the four** aspects are welded into one…the spark…caused by the Breath of Life itself!*

And in this moment, the First stage of Life…

Life Energy came into being!

This was the very First Christ Event…
Unity, first dividing Itself…the Sacrificing of its own being, for the sustaining and containing of its creation…
THE FIRST CAUSE,
The "Immaculate" Conception itself…
The Causal, Redemptive Virgin Mother.

God As Mother

God as Mother? It kept repeating itself in my mind, as if hearing an echo, remembered from some ancient past. It was then that I wondered if the visions of St. Bernadette were the Cosmic Mother herself? When the priests asked who this apparition was, St. Bernadette replied, the "Lady." She didn't say, the Virgin Mary, for the apparition called herself the Immaculate Conception. The "Lady" didn't say she *had* an Immaculate Conception, she said she was the Immaculate Conception – the first cause – the virgin birth of the universe. Could the visions of the children from Medjugorje[14] be the same? Could this be yet another example of the Cosmic Mother revealing herself to mankind?

It felt like something deep inside me had been reawakened from a dream. For hours we were held spellbound as Marie guided us through an understanding of what she unveiled as the *Generation of Number,* the nine stages and steps taken by the Cosmic Mother before creation – before the evolution of the universe – which we refer to as the *Big Bang.* This work unveiled the origins of eternal time – and its birth (differentiating of space), as *eternity* in the heavenly regions and *Time* in the lower form regions of cosmic space existence. We watched Primordial Matter unfold.

It went on and on…Marie's teachings illuminated the path, ignited the pattern, through which I entered into a pure state of awareness…I watched space contract as the Four Aspects, lying within the womb of the Cosmic Mother, began to divide into self-individualized states of living. Three of Her (masculine) aspects become the **three-in-one being of the Cosmic Trinity Creator** and the fourth aspect; Her purely self-less (feminine) Love Awareness…becomes…the **first Virgin Soul.**

---

[14] City in Yugoslavia where some children witness the apparitions of a majestic lady.

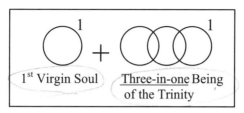

1st Virgin Soul   Three-in-one Being of the Trinity

First division of the One: (one can only divide itself by one)

The Cosmic Virgin Mother finally gives birth as the Big Bang, and Creation comes into being.

The great androgynous Causal Being has become the Macrocosmic Virgin Mother of the Cosmic Trinity Creator. By giving birth, She has now become creatively exhausted...for She – *God As Mother* – has sacrificed its own being, for *its* creation:

> *Her Spirit is found within the Trinity Creator;*
> *Her Soul, within the Virgin Soul;*
> *Her body will become creation.*

Marie went on to explain that there can only be nine stages and steps to creation, because there are only nine fundamental numbers in the numerical system. Using the Roman numerals as the symbols for the nine fundamental numbers:

X is ten...Ex –is –tence!

On the tenth step, *existence actually comes into being!*

The 'holy diversity' of the Pythagoreans, called the tetractys:

$$1+2+3+4=10$$

*Progress from oneness to the number four and the ten emerges, the **mother** of all things.*

– Pythagoras

Here is a quote from St. Thomas describing pre-Big Bang, before the division, where feminine and masculine are one:

When you make the two into one,
when you make the inner like the outer
and the outer like the inner,
and the upper like the lower,
when you make male and female into a
single one,
so that the male will not be male
and the female will not be female,
then you will enter the kingdom."
St. Thomas, Saying 22

Understanding the Language

It became increasingly difficult to think of nothing else but the implications of her work. There were so many aspects of it to understand.

One evening, I pulled out my tape recorder and reviewed one of our sessions on the *Causal Redemptive Virgin Mother.* I understood the word, "Causal" as:

The first Principle – that from which all else had come. I understood her use of the word "Virgin" to mean:

A pure state – selfless…no ego/self in it
But what did she mean by the word "Redemptive?"

I looked up at the clock. It was 2:30 a.m. I knew I wasn't going to get any sleep until I could figure this one out, so I decided to look it up in the dictionary. My general dictionary said: "to redeem, make up for, fulfill, rescue, liberate." But somehow, it didn't quite strike a cord with the way she had used it. I checked another dictionary and it said about the same. Then I remembered; I had a hundred-year-old dictionary in my library, downstairs.

I quietly turned the pages looking for the word, "redemptive." When I found it, the definition was lengthy, almost taking up an entire page. Starting at the top, it was basically the same definition I'd found in the other dictionaries. But just as I was about to give up, the last few lines caught my eye... *atonement, one who redeems himself.* And under that it said, *to suffer, to be forfeited by and to sacrifice.*

It was then that I thought, maybe this great Being had to sacrifice Itself, made to suffer or forfeited Itself...so life could come into being. And because this being was a *redeemer* and creator, it would have to take what was already there (because there is nothing else but itself), and *recreate* it – a First Cause.

Then I considered its Latin root, *redemptio:* meaning "buying back." Did Marie mean that this Being then needed to *buy back* or pay for and eventually *bring back* its creation to its original state? And was the price for bringing back its creation, long enforced and painful delay of its return?

She had described this Being as having four aspects. However, after listening to the tape over again, I heard her mention that one of the four was *selfless (self-less)* without self, or ego, which is limitless, not limited by the self. She also mentioned that the act of redemption is not only restoring or saving, but *must be love-motivated* within a purely selfless state. So in this body of work, the act of restoring or saving had become a part of the act of selfless-love.

The Journey

My journey had begun. Each day I'd work at the bookstore for a few hours then gather my things and set off for Marie's. There I was, dragging my notebook, papers, tape recorder, and video machine – I had so much equipment that I had to make two trips to the car just to unload. Sometimes others would join me. But most of the time, Marie and I were basically alone, talking about life, her work, and the mysteries of the universe – always with my tape recorder running. We would be in casual conversation, when she would suddenly begin to say something incredibly profound. And she would go on for hours. There was no way I could remember everything. Besides, there were certain things she would never repeat. It was as if, just for that moment, I could peer into the miracles of life, to hear the thoughts of God – then suddenly, the door would close and her words were never to be heard again.

Each day, after our daily walks, we would work on her fourth book. I would read each line to her, she would make her corrections, and I would type them in. At first, I couldn't understand her – questioning and challenging concepts that didn't make sense to me. In fact, sometimes I'd ask her so many questions, that I think I made her nervous. And if I got too excited, she would stop our session and have me work on something else. She said she wanted to keep me balanced – so she would send me off to the files. And there I'd sit in the office alone, shaking my head, questioning how on earth could she have developed all of this and sustained it?

Aside from my seeing her during the day, Marie had gathered a study group. This group, joined with the *core group,* who met a couple of evenings a week. Each time we gathered, we were like children at a campfire – all excited about being there, our minds young and undisciplined. When she began with describing Bruton Vault, we were all wide-awake, totally aware. But as she would continue, into the Cosmogony, no matter how hard we fought to stay focused, our minds would soon tire and begin to shut down from overload.

"It had to happen," Marie explained, "so that your Soul-mind could be left alone, awakened to receive."

110

The process of understanding was slow. At first, I could only listen to her for about ten or fifteen minutes. But as time went by my length of concentration grew. I gradually began to understand why she used words so differently...she had to take conventional words to describe things that had never been described before. New meanings had to be infused into the old – the English language was being forced to evolve.

These new words became *keywords*. Though unfamiliar to us, if continually repeated, these words would begin to unlock or activate the pattern that lay deep within our Souls. This pattern, once activated, would then trigger memories collected in the Soulmind from the many incarnations of the individual (programmed into the DNA). In other words:

Keywords (its shape and sound) act as a bridge
for the natural-mind to have access
to the memories of the Soul.

This re-conditioned Natural Mind, upon seeing or hearing these keywords (because of their shape, sound, or intonation) could now resonate with any new in-coming information, allowing a deeper layer or meaning to be revealed.

However, an even more difficult barrier to understanding the work existed.... *nothing was ever given in a linear order.* We sat there mesmerized on a Soul level, yet completely confused on a rational level. Her way of teaching and writing was completely against our natural order of thinking and reason; a frustrating experience for us all.

Then suddenly, one night, I recognized a clue! She had just given a lecture on the nature of space, when she repeated something that I had heard before, but never really absorbed. Since day one she had insisted, "But you first have to know about...this..." or "...first you have to know about.... that." This was it! Little did I know that this was her way of telling us what the true order was? *The reason:* She wanted us to be enlightened from within.

Our work was putting the pieces together. She had warned us:

> The process of collecting outside information, as in reading books, was "initiation from without." This would merely make us receptive to enlightenment into the great Wisdom of Love. It could not, and was never meant to bring us to enlightenment – it was merely to prepare us. Only " initiation from within" holds the key.

For she revealed:

> True enlightenment unto the Great Truth, the "True Wisdom of Love for All Life and All Living," must be achieved through personal experience – distilled from within and experienced by the Soul. These essences distilled and built up from that experience goes into the building of that Soul...and it is these essences that are carried in the memories of the Soulmind into other incarnations.

This was why, she explained, we could read every book, listen to every speech, but unless we have *personally* experienced an aspect of that truth, or personally relate to it in some way, it cannot be *absorbed* into the Soul. And if it is not absorbed by the Soul, the information is either forgotten, or stored in the *natural* mind, where it cannot be taken onto our next lifetime:

> *Our natural-mind (supported by the brain) along with its memories is bound to the physical form. At death, when the*

112

physical body dissipates, the physical body along with the natural memories are returned to the very make-up of the body and mind of the Earth from which it had come...but our Soulmind, will live on through eternities.

Upon finding this clue to the order of her thoughts, I was filled with joy. The work became my journey, and I shared with the others the clues I had found.

Each of us was drawn to Marie for different reasons, and the different aspects of the work became food for our Souls. I can't say how the others felt, but I knew I had found my own Life's Assignment...a path that would lead me to a Truth. Marie would later call this "Dreaming True," and because I was privileged to have had the time to study with her, I vowed to share whatever I gleaned from the work, with anyone who wanted to listen.

Breakthrough

Our small core group was determined. We all went on a reading binge going through all of her books and then returned for our weekly meetings with questions in hand. I started a glossary; slowly the language began to come alive. Everyone collected the bits and pieces of information, but like gems strewn upon the beach, they had to be separated from the sand. The process of understanding her work was slow – frustrating. So I decided to take matters into my own hands; there had to be another way.

I started off by reading along with the others, taking notes, but when I went to bed, I set my tape recorder to my ear, replaying Marie's private lectures allowing her voice to lull me to sleep. Her words would permeate my mind. I'd found the key…this was the process that conditioned my mind to her language and her speech.

The tapes went on, while I drove to and from work, during lunch breaks, any time I could spare – listening and re-listening with very little understanding. Yet there were clues that something was happening. I began to recognize speech patterns and concepts that she had applied with consistency. I studied her use of phraseology and contextual clues imbedded in her message....and found Ariadne's thread, the fundamentals or basic language of the work!

I then began to transcribe the tapes that now filled my file drawers. At first, I did it manually – tape in one hand while writing and turning it on and off with the other. I was frustrated, even shaky after an hour or so, but I forced myself to concentrate, to memorize longer sentences. I fine-tuned my mind to hear her every word.

One day something extraordinary happened, while I sat alone in the dim light with my work spread out across the table. I had gone through four or five tapes, looking for pieces of information regarding the origin of matter. Not finding what I needed, I looked at the stacks of tapes and randomly pulled one from the bottom of a stack.

Amazingly, I had randomly pulled the exact tape filled with the missing information to complete my notes. It was one of those experiences that would continually repeat itself during the writing of this book – an affirmation or presence of a higher power at work...as though God had placed the things I was searching for, into my very hands.

On this tape, Marie described the *origin and nature of time,* and how time substance enters matter. As I concentrated on transcribing, I soon found myself experiencing a shift into a completely different dimension...

Suddenly, I was watching life, as if seeing it through God's eyes...everything became crisp and clear...was this, the eye of the

Soul? It felt as if my mind was huge. There was a sense of added depth or dimension that even now I struggle to explain. I could clearly sense a vastness, yet at the same time, I was aware of the smallest particles most close to me – it appeared as if space had inverted into itself, to create more space within its three-dimensions. It grew dark and silent – I could hear the tape, no more. I saw atoms flying through space...molecules and its layers, one built upon another as the universe contracted and expanded before me. I saw life enter energy, moving it forward, to become the positive aspect of force. And as this energy moved over space, space became curious – for nothing had moved across it before. This curiosity became the negative aspect of force, a time substance that moved with energy, sustaining it long enough for my eyes to see.

It seemed as if I was watching for eternity, when suddenly, I gasped for air! I came out of the trance taking a deep breath...I had forgotten to breathe! I pushed myself away from the table. I'd gone too far – too deep. Getting up, I started to sway. It wasn't dizziness – it was more like a feeling of expansion. I felt like a great giant peering into a miniature world. Everything looked so small and insignificant around me. And although this view was at first unnerving, I became curious and began to find this new state quite exhilarating. This momentary vision had initiated a shift in my consciousness to where I had moved into a pure and somewhat lasting state of awareness, of being.

I remembered that Marie had explained that the quickest way to connect the awareness of our Soulmind, with the consciousness of the spiritmind and the brain of the Natural mind, was through audiovisual means...eliciting the hearing and the seeing of the mind at the same time. Was this what I had done? Did I activate the audio through listening to the tape, and the visual by seeing the words transcribed, manifested upon the paper as I wrote?

Excited with this new knowledge, I yearned to share it with someone. As I went out into my garden in search of a human connection, I felt the concrete walkway up against my feet. When I looked down, the ground seemed so far away, yet I was aware of the tiniest particles that made up the concrete itself. There was a strange and puzzling spatial quality to the three dimensional landscape before me.

Needless to say, the intensity of this experience had lasted for quite some time…and as I sat there in the garden, I wondered if it could be repeated.

Back to Work

My back ached from bending over my notes as I pieced together the detailed information. I had finally acquired a transcribing machine and moved more quickly now. I watched as the *hidden* became unhidden; the *unknowable* had now become the *unknown* – to be known. And gradually, I began to stay alert whenever Marie spoke. I began to remember the things I had heard on tape and compared them with what she was saying. I had begun to understand her – and I shared each remarkable step with my colleagues…my true friends.

Things started to come together. When Marie spoke about the evolution of form and the involution of spirit, I began to understand: these were the two different generations that came to ensouling. Form evolved to ensouling by moving through the kingdoms,…from the ground up. She called this *form evolution:* from Mineral, to Plant, to Animal, to (the missing link) "Pre-human Animal-man," to human ensouling. The Spirits, evolved to ensouling by descending from the heavens to be quickened within the human form. This was called *spirit involution.* These included the Angelic Selfhoods and the mythological archetypes of the Gods & Goddesses (detailed later).

Marie explained that one could generally figure out from which direction they had come to ensouling by observing their own personality. If a person was self-centered, unusually arrogant or ego driven, they more likely evolved from the strong-willed spirits that *descended* from the heavens. A mild or gentle individual would generally have *ascended* upward through the kingdoms of form (mineral, plant, animal, etc.).

For three years, I immersed myself solely into the work, collecting information from before the Big Bang to existence itself. But it wasn't until the middle of the third year that I thought to go through the files to see if all my notes were complete and in order. I was worried and exhausted...so much work. So much time had passed. What if something was missing? If so, I wasn't sure if I could go on. There I sat, looking at my computer – frozen, intimidated by the magnitude of the work. Now, I had to shift from collecting the information to sharing what I'd found. This meant I had to commit to writing a book.

That day I decided to look over what I had been piecing together for years. I pulled out the glossary that I had developed to organize Marie's ideas and looked up the Generation of Number. Page by page, I held my breath and counted the steps through...then finally, I saw step 9, and then Roman Numeral X (Ten), *Existence came into being!* The entire nine stages and steps, which the Causal Being would take towards its own transformation as the great Causal Mother, lie within my computer, waiting to be unveiled. For the first time, I could follow each delicate step, sifting through its disorienting repetition to find a clear, sequential order to the Causal Mother's act of creation.

I sat spellbound. It didn't matter that it still needed to be edited...the information was finally, *all* there.

The Diagrams

This was the moment I'd been waiting for. Now that I had all the stages and steps of Creation, I could embark upon the deciphering of those mysterious diagrams Marie had isolated in the basement of her house. I pulled out the Xerox copies of the originals, and for days sat at my easel carefully scrutinizing each copy I had on hand. What did they all mean? Why did she draw them?

I had questioned Marie a number of times, but she was reluctant to speak of this part of her work. Driven and obsessed, she would forget to eat. She felt that the intensity of this systematic concentration was what had thrust her into a coma.

Marie did offer one detail: at the core of each diagram was a cross, overlaid by an X. She said that it was always at the core of the diagrams and could be confirmed by the light emanating from the birth of a star. She had discovered one of the first photographs taken at the Griffith Park Observatory that marked this event: the light emanating from the birth of a star had the same pattern.

For days I sat with my magnifying glass analyzing the small writings surrounding each diagram, trying to make things out. Then one day, as I was casually speaking to someone on the phone, I unconsciously started doodling – drawing circles within circles and lines that connected to other lines. After hanging up, I began to focus on what I'd drawn, and was stunned to see the geometric designs of the diagrams manifested before me…except now, the meanings of the mysterious diagrams had begun to be take form. I thought, "Could the upper three circles I had drawn, represent the Trinity Creator? Were the lower three, what was left behind, as they were being formed?" I pulled out one of my favorite diagrams I had seen in one of her books. (See diagram: Existence). On some unconscious level I had duplicated it, there were my three circles, intertwined. Then I noticed a large "X" near the top of the page of Marie's diagram. X? I remembered X-is-Ten, I counted the lines, attributing them to the Generation of Number and symbols to the steps of creation.

I started from the central line then counted the lines that went up to the top – *there were ten!*

This was it – Everything in the cosmology, and each of the ten stages and steps were geometrically drawn as diagrams – there it lay unfolding before my eyes. I pulled out another diagram, the one with four circles interlocking. I could see! The four circles intertwined, symbolizing the four aspects of the Cosmic Mother's being, before they were individualized as the Trinity Creator, Virgin Soul and Creation!

I hurried to my easel, inspired by classical music playing on the radio behind me. I had been studying these diagrams for days, and now I was compelled to draw them. I chose one of the simpler looking diagrams that read "**Cosmic Conceiving**." Here I could see the four circles drawn quite clearly. I remembered my notes. Marie said she had started by drawing the "X" and the cross in the center of the blank paper, working from the center design of the diagram out.

While in college, I had studied architectural drawing – the lines of the diagrams felt natural to me. Following her diagram, I drew each line she drew; each line would guide me to the placement of the next. I used my compass to measure the width of the circles on her original, and then copied them onto my paper. Because *each item evolved into the next,* if a circle or line were off, I would erase it all and start again. It was the pattern that revealed the true order and how it should be aligned.

Hours went by. I was entranced by the patterns that lay before me. I slowly moved into a deep meditative state, loosing all sense of self. I don't know how many hours I'd been sitting there, but when I emerged, becoming conscious of my surroundings, I looked down at my drawing – the diagram was done! The radio station I was listening to earlier was now playing Gregorian

Chants. I felt as if there were angels standing all around me. How I did it, or how I finished the diagram, I'll never know.

Then something even more amazing happened. Looking up from the diagram, I noticed having the same feeling of expansion I had experienced before, in the garden. However, this time, as I looked about me, I could see the pattern of the drawing I had worked on, in the make-up of *everything* around me! There it was, the pattern – in the windows, the cabinets, walls and the floor. As I walked outside there it was again, that same pattern repeated over and over again – in the plants and trees within *all of nature!* Tears came to my eyes…I began to wonder…

Could these patterns be the thoughts of God made manifest, not as text, but as the intricate geometrical patterns and shapes that danced before me?

Were these lines the avenues through which Life and intelligence entered matter…summoning the atoms and molecules to the servitude of existence…creation?

Marie had said: *The Father aspect of the Trinity, created the Mind of Nature to permeate the mindless primordial matter, infusing nature with an "intelligence" – through which it could communicate with the mind of God. The Trinity, using the Mind of Nature, could then transmit his thoughts and ideas, influencing the elements, skillfully weaving them into the intricate patterns of organized form.*

Marie had used these geometrical diagrams as part of, what she believed to be, the natural evolution of writing…the next step…unhampered by the limitation of language or creed, whose secrets would become rewards to the man or woman who would diligently seek.

❖

The Book

As I began the arduous task of editing the massive amounts of material in my computer, my mind grew sharper; my concentration increased beyond my own belief. As Marie skipped about the Universe from one step to another, I was now able to follow. My psychic abilities were intensified; I could hear people's thoughts and know things before they happened. My dreams became lucid. And in the darkness just before the dawn, the teachings began. Things I didn't understand during the day would be revealed in my dreams at night. However, no matter how I tried to simplify and convey what I had been learning within *The Arcanum*, I soon came to the painful realization it was easier said, than done.

Every time I started to write, thinking that I was simplifying the work, people would look at me as if I were speaking another language. "I don't understand," they would say. For some reason, I just couldn't bring it through. I knew it in my head, but it hadn't merged with my heart. Feeling like a failure, I put the work down.

It had been a long, demanding journey. I was exhausted and was in need of a rest. For six months, I returned to my painting to renew my Spirit and reconnect with my Soul. But everywhere I looked the essence of *The Arcanum* was there too – opening up a different meaning – adding a new dimension to the images on my canvas, the books I read, or movies I'd see. And as I painted, my mind was torn in two... wavering between the two different courses my life could take – my art or writing.

Then one night after going through painstaking deliberation I had unconsciously induced a notable experience:

As I dozed off...I felt myself rise from my body and was suddenly thrust through the air. I was being guided by some invisible force, moving me quickly, yet deeper into space. It was magnificent; I could see the stars and the planets speeding by.

Suddenly, I found myself in a world quite similar to our own, yet the colors were far more vivid and inviting. I could feel the wind pressing gently against my skin as I sped through the air, floating down a road covered by trees that lined each side. Everything felt so alive. I laughed as I reached into the air to catch the large, beautiful green leaves that fell from the trees around me.

When I landed, there was a large meeting going on – modern people, wearing long Greek gowns and Roman-like tunics. Then I noticed that a few were wearing the very same large green leaves that I carried within my hands – except they had tied them within their clothing.

When I looked closer at the people with the leaves, I noticed that they all had numbers inscribed upon their clothing, written in gold, across their chests… 4 x 4, 5 x 5, etc. It reminded me of Marie's work where she used the 3 x 3 or Nine Stages and Steps to define the origins of the universe. I asked a young man wearing the leaves, what the 5 x 5 meant, and to that he replied, "It's part of the mysteries."

At that moment, I was curiously compelled to look upon my own chest – but no sooner had I realized that I had been given "3 x 3" – and that each who bore leaves had been given a piece to the puzzle of life – I found myself thrust back into my body.

When I finally opened my eyes, I knew just what to do – I was infused with an intense yearning to complete the task at hand.

So I went back – back to what I now knew was the beginning – the Generation of Number…for until I completed my life's assignment, there would be no peace of mind.

Upon returning to the book, I noticed that if my work at any time became self-serving, its secrets became unobtainable! The intent of sharing it with others had to remain pure. So I set my mind to break down the work always bearing this in mind.

❖

The Parallels Within the Arcanum and Science

One night while reading the book *Hyperspace*, by Michio Kaku, I was taken by surprise. The author explained that before the *Big Bang*, our world was a perfect ten-dimensional universe. Marie had written that the universe was created in nine stages and steps, along with the first nine dimensions. On the tenth step, *Existence actually comes into being,* along with the tenth dimension.

In Kaku's book, he continues to explain that this ten-dimensional Universe eventually cracked in two – splitting space somewhere between the fourth and sixth-dimension. In Marie's Arcanum, written in 1938, she writes: "during the fourth step, the Cosmic Mother contracts, pulling all her consciousness, intelligence and living (from all of space) to give to the Trinity Creator, within her womb." This left the deprived primordial matter in the lower regions where it was taken away. This "contracting" reconditioned (split) space into two regions, giving birth to eternal time, "differentiated as eternity in the upper regions and time in the lower four dimensions of space."

God As Mother

I had run across some information on Quantum Physics and it began to appear to me that many of Marie's symbols and ideas of how the universe was created written in 1938, were extraordinarily similar to contemporary ideas surrounding Superstring Theory.

Where science explains that all phenomenon in our universe can be reduced to four forces, I compared it to what Marie called, the original four aspects of God's being. And although still a theory, its uncanny resemblance to Marie's work was astonishing. Three of the forces (working closely together) appeared to have the same qualities as the Cosmic Trinity Creator. And the fourth force, Gravity (the illusive graviton) seemed to have the qualities of the Soul Nature that sustains them – lying invisibly (absorbed) from within (the dark matter).

In the book, *God and the Big Bang*, it was stated that following the Big Bang, the Universe was *exhausted*. Marie had said that on the tenth step, the Cosmic Mother "gave up" all her creative ability to the sustaining of the Trinity Creator – so after giving birth, the Cosmic Mother was left creatively exhausted. When a recent article theorized that light was thought to be a vibration in the fifth dimension, I wasn't surprised. Marie stated in her work, 50 years ago: Life "V" (5th step) is a five-dimensional aspect. And "since Life (heat) cannot be separate from light" she said, "they are both five-dimensional aspects."

❖

FINAL TRANSLATION

Following my own study of comparative religions, I have come to the conclusion that at the core they are all one and the same. I have also found that within this universal core lies a pattern that is duplicated within our Souls. It is a blueprint of the origin purpose and destiny of creation – lines of Life intelligence that wait to be ignited in understanding.

Innately, we go in search of the answers like explorers in search of the illusive truths. Sometimes we are guided from one belief system to another; other times we stay with one. And though I have embraced and practiced many aspects within the various belief systems, I have chosen to use my birth religion, Christianity as my home base. Yet knowing that there is much more, like an explorer, I am compelled to continue my search.

I was once asked during a radio broadcast, "If a person gives up traditional beliefs, to the extent that you have, then to whom are we personally accountable to?"

"God," I said, "the heart of my being...myself, my Soul."

"This troubles me." (Host)

"Why?" I asked.

"Because there needs to be a separation between God and the Soul of man. That way man could feel personally accountable to something other than himself." (Host)

To this I replied, why must I be motivated by accountability when I can be motivated by my love for God and the *aspiration* of being at one with the Divine. I later emailed him:

God can never be separated from man...the image cannot be separated from the original...

If you are the original, and you stand before a mirror,
you will see your image.
If you, the original, walks away from the mirror,

your image will cease to be.
Therefore God the original
cannot be separate from its image...man.

God as Mother

For many of us today, the concept of God, as Mother, is difficult. However, the feminine face of God is deeply rooted within the core of many religious teachings. A female divinity is found in Sumer, Babylon, Egypt, Africa, Australia and China[15] – from Ameratsu and Cannon in Japan, to Quan Yin in China – Tara in Tibet, Akua'ba in Africa – the Cosmic Mother in Egypt, and Ishtar and Astarte of the Middle East. Spider Woman; Ixchel the Weaver emerged in North America while the Mayas of Mexico celebrated the Cosmic Mother. The Hindu called Her, Divine Mother, and we speak of the Great Mother of the Tao. In Judaism's Kabala, we find Binah the uppermost feminine element. And now within Mystic Christianity and the revelation of the *Arcanum* we can find both the Cosmic Mother and the Great Goddess.

This Divine Mother, as the Supreme Being, cannot be ignored. Appearing from 40,000 BCE to 5,000 BCE, we find the Goddess as the primary deity. In fact, there are no images that have been found of a Father God throughout the prehistoric record.[16]

The feminine face of God not only reflects the deep seeded beliefs of our ancestors, but it is encoded in the bloodlines of humanity and cannot be erased.

Just as the human fetus is first feminine, with the masculine lying within a potential state waiting to unfold, it is here

---

[15] Merlin Stone, "When God Was a Woman."
[16] For more information see the book *White Goddesses,* by Robert Graves.

we see the Cosmic Mother giving birth to the masculine aspects of Her being...*As above, so below.*

This Arcanum is not about eliminating the masculine aspects of God; it is, for the Western mind, about acknowledging and embracing the feminine – unearthing our history and heritage.

I had a vision where I was given a card that read: You have written the book because She is the feminine that you longed to be. It was true...It was the *feminine* I had *disconnected* from, in order to survive...the feminine filled with love, no worries, no expectations. She is a selfless intelligence always sharing Itself – in whose arms we find a place where there is no regret, no pain no anguish...just peace. Simply being.

When I expressed these feelings to my husband he asked, "Then why the masculine?" to which I replied: the masculine is the creative principle, and without it there would be no creation. It also creates the circumstances through which we may evolve...it creates the heat that transforms and purifies...it carries the supernal light of the creative consciousness, that once transformed, unites with her Divine Love – by which we are set free.

Mystery of the Number Four:

From the One came Two; giving birth to the Three.
The Masculine lies within the Three or Creative Principle
The Feminine lies within the Four or Love Principle,
which sustains and contains the three.

Just as the core beliefs within a religion cannot be taken out without destroying the religion itself, so it is with the feminine face of God; for SHE **IS** LIFE, WHOSE NATURE IS LOVE – and cannot be taken away from us, without destroying the essence of whom we are, and from where we have come forth...the *MOTHER.*

God As Mother

What follows is an interpretive overview of the vast body of work Marie referred to as The Generation of Number, the Nine Stages and Steps to Ex-is-ten-ce...and the birth of the First Virgin Soul. Though I found her approach to be complex at times, I had realized that anyone trying to use written language to convey the invisible worlds of origins and causes would most certainly, come up deficient.

Here lies a synthesis of what I have learned over my own lifetime. It is a story of the hidden Mother of us all..."God beyond God."

The Vault has been opened, its light is our redemption: May the Wisdom of Love and Life understanding manifest and express itself within you through selfless and self-humbled service.

❖

To the property of motherhood belongs nature,
love, wisdom and knowledge and this is God...
speaking to Julian: I it am. The greatness and
goodness of the Father, I it am:
The wisdom and kindness of the Mother, I it am:
The light and grace that is all blessed love,
I it am...*Revelations of Divine Love* –
        Juliana of Norwich

Part IV

The
Arcanum

Part IV
Mystery of the Number Four:

THE
ARCANUM

3 x 3
Nine Stages and Steps to Creation

And the
Generation of Number

GENERATION
(III:IV)
X: (ENERGY:FORCE:FORM): REGENERATION : LIFE-LIVING : CAUSE OF LIVING
(I : II : III): (IV:III) : (V : VI) : (VII : VIII : IX) : X

Pre-Big Bang

Before Creation - During early, Cosmic Scale

There was no beginning, nor end…only the **One.**
And this One-ness had not yet become All-ness or All-encompassing as yet,
For there was nothing else but **Itself.**

This ancient cosmos existed before any world was, and the moment of creation was but a dream to come. Eternal-ness was not. Nor was there Eternity and Time, for energy and matter had not yet been conceived. It was a virgin state – formless, true and pure. Duality did not exist for all was the One.

However, space was…

> *Space had always existed*
> *Space was the immeasurable container of God's being,*
> *just as our bodies house our Souls.*

Guided Imagery:

Can you understand the *vastness* of this space?   Can you *feel* its depth? Imagine space as a container (or receptacle) that was infinitely changing, expanding and contracting to accommodate and *sustain,* that which it contained. Space would be boundless with an infinite variety of shape and multi-dimensional form.

Now close your eyes and slowly…imagine your hand reaching out into the depths of this space...stretching out...as far as the inner eye can see and then beyond. You can no longer see this hand...yet you know it's there. Move through this space...feel its vastness...experience the unlimited *presence* of that space...(not the energy – but the space that the energy will fill).

Now move in all directions, *feeling the space that you move through*. Stretch out even farther...go yet deeper into its darkness – until, like a blanket, it envelops you…and at every point of your being you are filled with its dark warmth of Love.

As your hand returns – experience the space you move in. And when you walk across the room, remember to feel and concentrate on the space that *you* are taking up as you walk. Remember this experience so that you may understand the nature of God, our Eternal Parent wrapped in its invisible body, "Space."

There is no empty space...the nature of space is to contain...
God is space and space is the container of God's living
and being!

Space is filled with God's being:

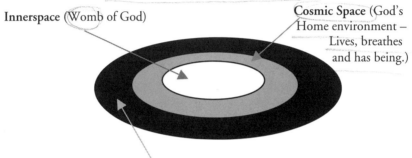

Innerspace (Womb of God)

Cosmic Space (God's
Home environment –
Lives, breathes
and has being.)

Cosmic Space Existence
This fills out to infinity. It is here that we will eventually
live, breathe and have *our* being.

And within God's being are four aspects
that fill all of space...

dark warmth of · Love

The Four Aspects of God's Being

According to science, everything in our Universe is made up of four forces, *Gravity, Electro-magnetic, Strong and Weak force.* These are said to contain magnetic or electric-magnetic influences:

The nature of magnetics is attraction: Love
The nature of electric is light: Consciousness

In this work, *God* has four aspects to its nature, differentiated though never divided, and filling all that is. They are:

- **The CAUSAL-BEING** (4th aspect is active): *FEMININE in nature & purely "magnetic" – we start with the fourth aspect, because its magnetic warmth sustains the other three*

- **The SELF-BEING** (1st aspect lies dormant): *MASCULINE in nature & "electric"*

- **The INTELLIGENCE-BEING** (2nd aspect lies dormant): *MASCULINE in nature & "electric"*

- **The ONE-BEING WITH SPACE (EXISTENCE)** (3rd aspect lies dormant): *MASCULINE in nature & "electric"*

(This is reflected in the human fetus, which is purely feminine for the first weeks of gestation, while the masculine lies in a potential or dormant state.)
NOTE: To skip details, move to summary on page 132.

The 4th Aspect of God:

Causal-Being

The Causal-Being, the only feminine aspect of God, is a pure **magnetic warmth.** It lies fully in one aspect (shaded area) while sustaining the other three masculine, electric aspects of Her being (white areas):

Causal Being
4th **Aspect**
(Shaded areas)

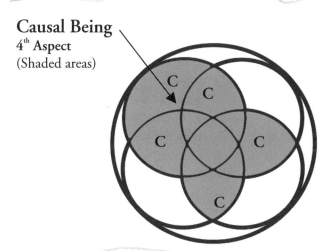

God is Life...whose nature is Love!

The **CAUSAL-BEING** (4th aspect) is the *true nature of God; it is pure **Love!*** This Causal-Being or Love is the Divine Principle from which all things are first caused. It not only *is* the **Essence of** LIFE, but also contains and sustains all Life thereafter. There is no "Self" (ego), within this Causal-Being ...only a pure **Self-less* Love.**

This Causal-Being, or *Love,* has an *intelligence* we call *Awareness.* This makes God a selfless *Love-Awareness* that

---

* The term "selfless," without self, is "limitless." It is the self that places limitations upon us. (in this language we can associate the term Selfless with the Eastern term "Self," with a capital S.)

completely fills this (Causal) aspect of *its being* and a *portion* of the remaining three aspects:

a) The purely magnetic warmth of the Causal Being (4ᵗʰ Aspect) overflows into the other three aspects:

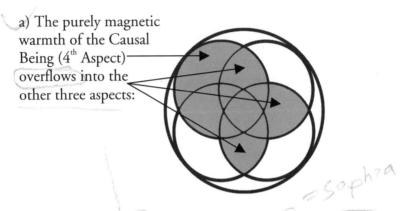

=Sophia

b) The completely shaded circle is the Causal Being, pure Love-Awareness. It is a feminine-magnetic warmth ingredient that pours into a portion of the remaining 3 unconscious, masculine and electric areas [in white] to sustain them.

The Causal-Being sustains *and replenishes* the other three aspects with Love, Life and eventually the Light (to ignite its consciousness [white areas] – now lying dormant in an unconscious state). And so it is with this Love-Awareness that God makes the other aspects of its being ever-living...*sustaining* the universe as a *magnetic-warmth* that becomes the matrix (or mother) of all matter that is later manifested:

> *This Causal-Being, this Love-Awareness*
> *is the purely **feminine** aspect of God*
> *that will later through sacrifice:*
> *be consumed by the heat of its Love, ALONG with*
> *the remaining three aspects of its being,*
> *and welded into the first ingredient of Life.*

The Causal-Being is a God of selfless Love – not of a creative nature (though it lies potent), but a causal nature, that will recreate and reform Its own Being, into a new life.

Here is revealed the hidden meaning of the numbers "Three" and "Four." Later, when Creation begins, and God recreates its being for the first time, these four aspects are first divided as 1 + 3:

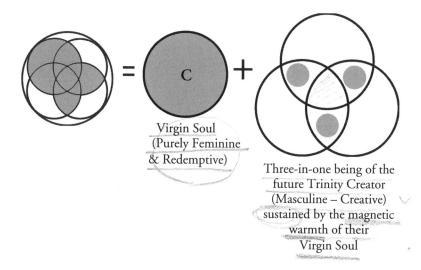

Virgin Soul
(Purely Feminine
& Redemptive)

Three-in-one being of the
future Trinity Creator
(Masculine – Creative)
sustained by the magnetic
warmth of their
Virgin Soul

Unity first dividing itself…
The One can only divide itself by itself.
That's why the Trinity is known as a three-in-*one* Being

The "1" Causal-Being (feminine) becomes the first **Virgin Soul** to be born – while the remaining "3"(masculine) become the **three-in-One** Being: Father, Son, and Holy Spirit, the future **Trinity** Creator.

The Virgin Soul is a pure state that has no self in it, hence Self-less Love – and it is its unlimited Love-Awareness that becomes the Intelligence that flows through the Soulmind of every Soul.

Examine the numerical construction of the DNA molecule, which has four constituents at its base. These combine into sets of three...the elusive One is absorbed by the remaining three, so that they may be sustained...*As above, so below!* This can also be compared to the attributes of the four forces that govern the Universe, Gravity, Electro-magnetic, Strong and Weak force. Could the illusive graviton, within the force of Gravity be compared to the illusive Causal Being that has been absorbed into its creations?

"The Four Mighty Ones are in every man."
...William Blake

These *Four Mighty Ones* may also be compared to the four Hebrew characters "YHWH," which form the four-lettered mystery-name of the creative Power...it is said that creation unfolds from within the four. In alchemy we find it within the 'axiom of Maria Prophetissa; and for Jacob Bohme, the Tetragrammaton is an expression of the trinity... "The unity when the J. goes into itself into a threefold being...to an active life."

The 1st Aspect of God:

⸢ Self-Being

The Self of God
(One of the three Masculine parts of God)

The Self-Being is both *magnetic and electric*, because the magnetic awareness of the Causal Being (shaded area) is what sustains the dormant, electric (and unconscious) Self-Being (white area).

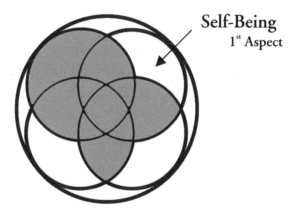

Self-Being
1ˢᵗ Aspect

The **SELF-BEING** (1ˢᵗ aspect) is the ***Spiritself** (Spirit* and *Self)* of God. The Self-Being imparts Self (and sustains and contains the Self of God in all three masculine parts:

SELF-Being

Where the **Causal**-Being (4th aspect) recreates Itself by nature and uses awareness for its intelligence, the **Self**-Being (1st aspect) is *creative* by nature, using *consciousness* for its intelligence. Consciousness ignites and lights up the Self's intelligence – using the same Life and Light ingredients or essences that we use for our existence.

However, the Self-Being of God, with its *creative consciousness,* is lying dormant within a deep sleep – an unconscious state. It is unconscious because it has used its life and light up, and must go into an unconscious state to replenish itself. This shows us how limited consciousness really is – for unless it can replenish itself, it will perish and become subject to death. This is why *we* sleep! The question is, what replenishes and sustains the Self Being's consciousness? The answer: It is the unlimited Love-Awareness of the Causal Being.

The Self-Being (1st), both masculine and creative by nature, is motivated by the pressure to create; therefore, it is the Self-Being that will later become the ***All-Conscious* Spirit** in the **Father** aspect of the Trinity Creator:

THREE-IN-ONE BEING OF THE FUTURE TRINITY CREATOR

Self-Being later becomes:
All-Conscious
FATHER

The 2nd Aspect of God:

Intelligence-Being

Intelligence of God
(The second of the three masculine parts of God)

The Intelligence Being is both magnetic and electric…
the magnetic Causal Being (shaded area) sustains the
(dormant) electric consciousness of the Self-Intelligence (white area).

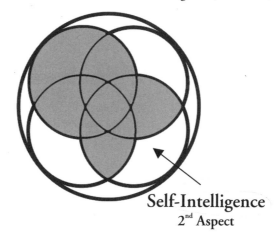

Self-Intelligence
2nd **Aspect**

The **INTELLIGENCE-BEING** (2nd aspect) is the *intelligence of God*. It imparts or gives intelligence, contains and sustains the intelligence nature of the Self of God, nourishing and instructing all three masculine parts:

INTELLIGENCE-Being

The **Intelligence**-Being (2nd aspect) is also **creative** by nature, using *consciousness* to ignite and light up its intelligence – And now we find the (electric) consciousness of both the:

Self-Being (1st aspect) & this **Intelligence-Being** (2nd aspect), is *lying dormant* within a deep sleep or unconscious state – while being sustained by the (magnetic) warmth of the Causal-Being (4th) and its Love-Awareness.

This Intelligence-Being, both creative and masculine by nature, is also motivated by the pressure to create: Therefore, it is the Intelligence Being (2nd aspect) of God that later becomes the *All-intelligent* **Spirit** in the **Son** aspect of the Trinity Creator.

THREE-IN-ONE BEING
OF THE FUTURE TRINITY CREATOR

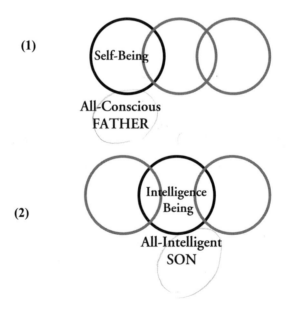

(1)

Self-Being

All-Conscious
FATHER

(2)

Intelligence
Being

All-Intelligent
SON

The 3rd Aspect of God:

Space-Being

Being and Space as One
(The third of the three masculine parts of God)

The Space-Being (3rd aspect) is both magnetic and electric. Its consciousness also lies dormant in an unconscious state (white area below), while being sustained by the (magnetic) awareness of the Causal-Being (1st aspect) (shaded area).

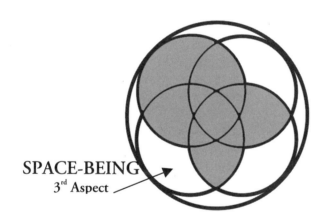

SPACE-BEING
3rd Aspect

T he *ever-living* SPACE-BEING (3rd aspect) is *God's being and space as **One**,* for space is the "container" of all of God's being – just as our bodies house our souls. The Space-Being creates, contains, and sustains (forming and re-forming) space in all four parts:

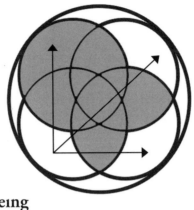

SPACE-Being
3rd Aspect

The Space-Being also includes the space we live and move in,
for it is within space that we share our being with God, as "One."

The **Space**-Being (3rd aspect) too is **creative** by nature, using *consciousness* to ignite and *light up* its intelligence. And so now we have the (electric) consciousness of all three masculine aspects of God, the:

> **Space-Being** (3rd aspect), Intelligence-Being (2nd aspect), and Self-Being (1st aspect), are *lying dormant* within a deep sleep or unconscious state – while being sustained by the (magnetic) warmth of the Causal-Being (4th) and its Love-Awareness.

The Space-Being, like the other two masculine aspects, being creative in nature, are motivated by the pressure to create. Therefore, it is the Space-Being, (3rd Aspect) of God that later becomes the ***All-living* Spirit** in the **Holy Spirit aspect** of the Trinity Creator.

THREE-IN-ONE BEING
OF THE FUTURE TRINITY CREATOR

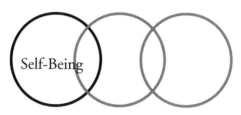

All-Conscious
FATHER

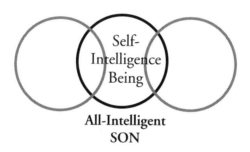

All-Intelligent
SON

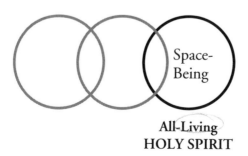

All-Living
HOLY SPIRIT

The Universal Concept:

> *With no beginning…*
> *God was an unconscious, yet* <u>*Love Aware-Intelligence*</u>
> *with* **four** *aspects to its nature – three were masculine,*
> *one was feminine.*

> *These four, were differentiated, but never divided…a composite*
> *of: Soul (Causal-being); Spirit (Self-being); Mind (Intelligence-*
> *being) and Body (Space-being).*

> *Its Spiritself resided in the three masculine aspects that lay in an*
> **unconscious** *state…*
> *while the Fourth, feminine aspect (Causal-being) remained*
> *Selfless (with no "self") and fully* **aware** *of its Love and Life*
> *dreams.*

> *…This androgynous Being, filled all of space.*
> *And all else thereafter, above and below*
> *was made, contained, and sustained by the* **"Four."**

And what was God doing?

God, this Intelligent Love-Awareness filling all of space, was…

> *SLEEPING…DREAMING…An awareness intelligence that*
> *lay sleeping –* **unconscious** *– though* **aware** *that within Itself, it*
> *filled the endless depths of space – filling it with a love-warmth*
> *that lay in a darkness waiting to be awakened…to creation.*

*DREAMING…in its unconscious, Loving-sleep. A **static** state… Dreaming of all its CREATIONS to come…throughout Eternity, Time and Space.*

*These were God's Love and Life dreams: dreams of **involution** – where God divides Its being into an infinite number of fractions; and dreams of form **evolution** – where God watches in anticipation as all unsouled and ensouled generations, living creatures, and creation perfect each aspect of their being – to return to the One.*

For only within the dreams could the One God lovingly share Itself with all of its creations…

*But God is aware that these are **only dreams**; this Oneness is a purely Self-less state…It **needs** to give! Its nature is to give, to share…with anyone, anything, **outside** Itself…*
Yet nothing else exists, but Itself!

*So the One begins to yearn… It yearns to realize these Dreams… so that it may truly give, truly love, by making these **Dreams a reality.***

We may think of this as the cause of the Big Bang – God's yearning, God's Selfless Love drawing the mass (heat) together:

This intense yearning is a Self-less Desire – a magnetic one – taking and drawing to Itself…consuming all that it is.
And within Its own flames of Love…Its Life and Light ablaze…burning, heating…It engulfs its own being…

Here, amidst Love's fire of supernal light, the One God perpetually "breathes in" its OWN aspects of its being…inhaling, *"transforming" and recreating these ingredients (darkly, magnetic-warmth radiations) into the **"Breath of Life"** itself.*

This breathing in [It's being], transforming it, and breathing out, sharing the Breath of Life, gave Being to space...reinforcing the Love (magnetic-warmth) of Its Causal-Being (4th), thus heat intensifying.[17] *For this is what it will take to build a new life...the Sacrifice of Its own being, for Its creation, the very first "Christ Event"... The first immaculate conception and origin of the **Virgin Birth.***

God has begun recreating It's own being – allowing Itself to be absorbed into the Fires of Life, to sustain Its very Creations. This is Unity, first dividing Itself. (There are two more Christ Events to come)...

This is likened to Einsof of the "Tree of Life," in the Kabala – the Infinite, "God beyond God." Some call It the "Great Nothingness," having been absorbed by Its creations, God appears not to be there...But God is there... always sustaining and containing all that is:

And as the Breath of Life continues to be transformed within the inner space or womb of God, the heat grows more intense. The desire to give its love, beyond what can be endured...

...Amidst the flames of Love...comes Its fateful cry, Let there be Life! Thus causing the welding of It's "four" Love sustaining (magnetic) ingredients of the Causal Being (4th), the core of God's being, to be chemically/alchemically welded into a newly formed state:

---

[17] The heat invokes the (magnetically sustained) consciousness (electric light factor) of a living state.

FIRST ENERGY
is manifested

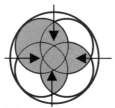

(The shaded areas are the feminine-magnetic Love ingredients that are
welded into the newly formed state of first energy.)

But this is not unconscious energy, for something must be
conscious before it can go unconscious...and if it is conscious then
it must be *alive.* Therefore, **First Energy is:**

Great Nothingness

the desire to give its love,
the flammed Love

I

LIFE ENERGY

Cosmic Redemptive Virgin Mother

The point at center is the beginning of Divine Life Energy weld into One from within the womb of God. Here the mass (heat) is brought together for the birth of the Generation within her (the origins of the Big Bang). The symbol of the cross represents the Cosmic Redemptive Virgin Mother... Unity, the One, first dividing Itself. This is the first step of the 9 stages and steps of creation.

Life Energy and the First Dimension Have Come to Manifest...

And out of the darkness and silence there came Life Energy... The first ingredient needed to engender a new life within Her womb! It was the first act of Love, the first step towards an All-Life and All-Living state.... God as Unity dividing Itself for the first time, sacrificing Itself for Its first creation.

God has now become the COSMIC MOTHER sharing her Energy her Life! This is the first division of her being... the First step...the first ingredient toward the sustaining of a new life within her womb.

God our Trinity Creator within Her womb [handwritten]

The shape of the cross (Mother) is similar to the fraction of one, "first" dividing itself:

$$\frac{1}{1} \quad +$$

This was the first Christ Event, the life of God sacrificed for Its creations.

The Cosmic Mother (the active, Feminine Aspect of being) was not creating, but redeeming/recreating Her own (masculine-creative) aspects…sacrificing herself out of Love…so that She may engender a new life from and within Her being.

(Binah in the Kabala may represent God our Trinity Creator within Her womb.)

Binah [handwritten]   *redeeming/(re)creat~* [handwritten]

At this point, the Cosmic Mother had anticipated that any creations of **matter** (physical, spirit matter, or otherwise) made from Her being, would need to be sustained. She was all there was, all-encompassing – and when She took the ingredients from one part of her being to recreate this new ingredient of Life Energy, it left a hole/vacuum, where it was taken away: Ø

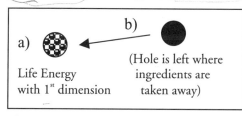

sustainable [handwritten]

a)
Life Energy
with 1st dimension

b)
(Hole is left where
ingredients are
taken away)

This hole needed to be sustained – otherwise the ingredients that were taken away, would automatically return to its original place – because there can be no empty space.

This also meant that the newly forming Generation within her womb, who received these new Life ingredients, also needed to be sustained…otherwise these new ingredients given to its makeup would seek to return to fill the hole from which it had come. So…

151

Along with the creation of First Life Energy, this love reaction caused the manifesting of the FIRST STAGE toward the birth of the Sustainer "Eternal Time," the beautiful Chimaera.[18] *Chimera is Eternal Time Herself...A Being created to serve the Cosmic Mother, in helping to sustain creation within her womb.*

With the creation of **Life Energy I,** is caused the **"energy" aspect of Eternal Time**, to sustain it (so it won't go back to fill the hole):

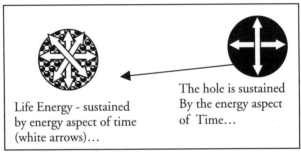

Life Energy - sustained by energy aspect of time (white arrows)...

The hole is sustained By the energy aspect of Time...

This **Energy aspect** of **time-substance** will help sustain the newly manifested **Life Energy** that lies within Her inner space — Her womb:

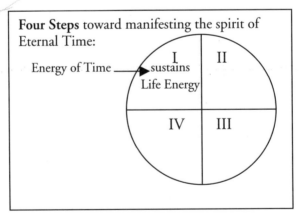

Four Steps toward manifesting the spirit of Eternal Time:

Energy of Time — sustains Life Energy

I   II

IV   III

---

[18] Chimera: is what Marie called Eternal Time.

And with Life Energy manifesting, along with the first stage toward the birth of Chimera (Eternal Time), the heat intensifies:

> *...The fierce flames of the Cosmic Mother's Love and Self-less desire to share and give that Love, causes an overflow of Love-warmth. The heat within the four parts of her Being (Causal Being [4th], Self-Being[1st], Intelligence-Being [2nd], and Space Being [3rd]) now welded, continues to rise...growing, permeating all aspects within space.*

> *And as the Cosmic Mother's Breath of Life reinforces this heat, her Self-Being (1st aspect) is stirred, and She begins to awaken from her deep sleep. This extra overflow of love warmth (gray area) IGNITES the unconscious "SELF-BEING" (1ST) white area...*

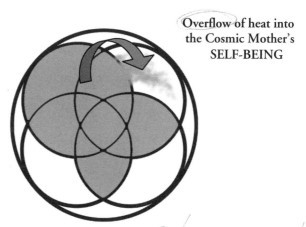

Overflow of heat into
the Cosmic Mother's
SELF-BEING

> *...bringing Her from an: unconscious to a SUBCONSCIOUS STATE!*

> *The origin of consciousness (white area) lies concealed in darkness, the Mother of Light (darkness gives birth to light). And it shall lie concealed in this darkness until love brings it forth – for consciousness is transformed by Love.*

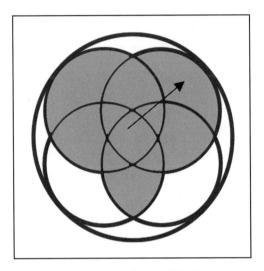

The subconscious waking of the first aspect:
The "Self" of God

In the SECOND STAGE of Her experiencing the engendering of a new life from within her womb, the Cosmic (Redemptive) Mother was fully aware that her **Self-Being** (1st) had begun its transformation from within:

And with Her awakening, the stillness of Life Energy is set into motion. Thus, the moving Life Energy becomes...LIFE FORCE!

II
LIFE FORCE

Origin of the Alphabet
(Length, height & depth)

Moving Energy Creating
the Circle

Life Force and the Second Dimension have come to manifesting… contained and sustained by and from within the Cosmic Mother's being!

Life Force…Energy in movement!
Stretching…Free…Moving across space it danced the dance of
Life… The energy of Life in wondrous movement…in perfect
accord.

It was all She had dreamed of…all she had wanted…
Stretched out before her, yearning to be more.
She cried in her sleep…Filled with Joy,
for her dreams were becoming a reality.

the dance
of
Life

And as this Life Energy moved across Space (the container of the Cosmic Mother's being), that Space became curious for nothing had moved there before.

Since space is an aspect of God's being it is filled with an intelligent *awareness*. When energy first moved across Space, this intelligent awareness, became **curious,** asking, "What is this, which moves over me?" Hence, the term *space curiosity*.

This space curiosity caused a second aspect of time-substance (the make-up of time) to form, which became the 2nd aspect of Eternal Time (Chimera) to be manifested within the Cosmic Mother's inner space or womb:

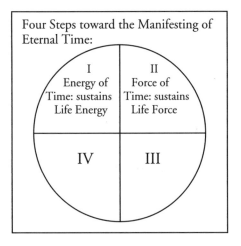

Four Steps toward the Manifesting of Eternal Time:

I — Energy of Time: sustains Life Energy

II — Force of Time: sustains Life Force

IV

III

Note: In Marie's Generation of Number, Energy is the first step toward building a new life within the Cosmic Mother's womb. When this energy begins to move across space, it becomes force – picking up or consuming the time substance along the way – the time substance stays in line with that moving energy measuring its motion and how far it can go. Therefore, **energy in motion** becomes the positive aspect of force and the time substance becomes the negative aspect of force.

The 2nd aspect of Eternal Time would "sustain" and carefully measure the Life Energy that danced throughout Her Space being.

And as Time measured the Life Energy being used…the Energy, alive with all its beauty, picked up just enough Eternal Time substance to sustain it along its way…

❖

But Her dreams continue…the intensity to give ever-growing stronger! AND AGAIN, as the pure, Self-less Love of the Cosmic Mother increases, so does the heat – and there is yet another overflow of Love warmth…

With Joy, the Cosmic Mother sacrifices still more of Her own being – And by embracing the flames of Love…
The extra overflow of Love warmth (gray area) IGNITES the subconscious "INTELLIGENCE-BEING" (white area):

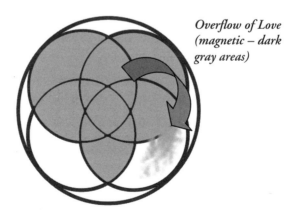

Overflow of Love (magnetic – dark gray areas)

…bringing her from a subconscious to a **CONSCIOUS STATE!**

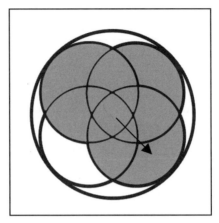

Consciousness transformed by Love

The Conscious waking of the second aspect:
The "Intelligence Being of God

This is the THIRD STAGE of Her experiencing the engendering of the glorious new life from within Her womb!

> *Yet within this conscious waking, the Cosmic Mother continues to mold Her Love and Life Dreams...perpetually sharing Her Breath of Life – watching as this moving energy, Life Force, runs out of time (substance) and comes to a halt...*

This moving energy stops in an energy-vacated point in space, initiating rotational movement (just as the essential components of nature):

> *And again, through Her love and sacrifice for the creation within, She then takes this Life Energy and Life Force (which is chemical - mixing these ingredients), and through an alchemical process (through Her Love), the Life Force II absorbs the Life Energy I (in reverse order)...and they are welded together in space, as one...becoming: The Three Principle of **LIFE FORM!***

III

The Creative Principle:

LIFE FORM

And the Third Dimension is manifested

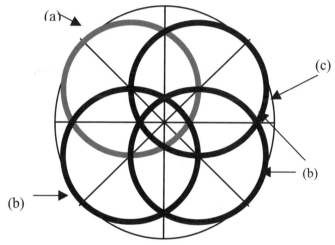

- *In the third stage, the four circles represent the Four Aspects of the Cosmic Mother being conditioned in space.[*]*

- *The lighter gray circle (a) represents the future feminine, 1st Virgin Soul; and the three darker circles (b), represent the future masculine, Trinity Creator. All fit neatly within the outer circle (c), representing the inner space or womb of God.*

Life Form III is not form, as we know it...

---

[*]Hence, this can be seen as the four forces within the makeup of the universe.

159

It is the thread the Cosmic Mother weaves throughout the fabric of form (matter). These veins, these avenues penetrate form, and like rivers, carry the essence of Life and intelligence throughout form... so it becomes a self-moving state:

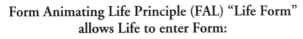

Form Animating Life Principle (FAL) "Life Form" allows Life to enter Form:

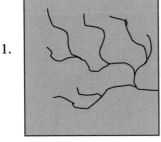 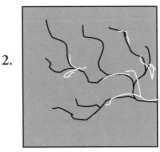

1. Life Form enters matter (gray), creating avenues (black).
2. Life (white) enters form through these avenues.

FAL Principle is not form itself, but the **"Animating Life Factor"** or 4th dimensional vehicle that penetrates 3 dimensional form, matter...carrying the 5 dimensional Life essences throughout 3 dimensional form. (A 5-dimensional aspect cannot directly enter a 3-dimensional aspect without going through the 4th.)

And as it weaves its way throughout matter (or form), it will reshape, reform, and reorganize matter into the body of a new form or life, a more evolved vehicle whose organs will eventually sustain consciousness and facilitate ensouling.

This ***Form Animating Life Principle (FAL)*** will become the tool, along with the essence of Life, which the Cosmic Mother uses to insure the transition of the Kingdoms (mineral, plant, animal...). This is because, Life Form III and the Essence of Life, both have an *innate need to evolve.* And once they penetrate form (or matter), even if that form is without consciousness or ensouling, it will automatically reorganize its composition, driving

160

that form on all levels (i.e. physical, spirit, astral, etheric), pressing it ever onward through its own evolution - thus providing a more *evolved vehicle* whose organs will eventually sustain consciousness and ensouling. (The web membrane-like surfaces are quite similar to what scientists call "branes," membrane-like surfaces that exist on various dimensions. See: Transition of the Kingdoms.) 📎

So as Life Form, Life's golden veins, winds Itself through form (matter), the Essence of Life will later course through these veins, and hand in hand, the two join making their way into form; thus causing form to become a Self-moving state.

*Form, once it is filled with Life, lives only to evolve...It evolves by providing greater and purer vehicles for the spirits of man and nature to develop within **their** incarnations. As living forms of all worlds and dimensions become the vehicles in which these spirits of man and nature incarnate, these forms are able to move towards reunification or a state of perfection. This is so ALL form and Life, suffering the longing to return, will eventually become One.*

Everything, form and Life, must return to the Source. And since the Cosmic Mother is the Source, she must eventually replenish Herself. But to do this, She will need to go into a state of rest. Just as *we* need to rest, to revitalize ourselves, so does the Cosmic Mother who waits in anticipation as we evolve (making Her one again) – for She cannot rest until She is made whole.

And nothing evolves without heat. Ahh, the heat...
drawn to us through our suffering, purifying us –
just as the sun and rain beat upon the soil
purifying the minerals of our future Earth,
that waits to be transformed.

161

And like alchemists,
our experiences will be the heat that shall burn away
the gross materials of our being…along with our misgivings,
leaving only the purest of essences,
used for the building of our Soul.

All this is so that we may return to a purified state…
to the One, our source…the Mother of us all, God.
And once all returns, She shall again, go into a state of rest –
where She may replenish and reform Herself,
only to reawaken…loving and yearning again and again.

This state of rest reflects the cycles of expansion and contraction of the universe. It allows the Cosmic Mother to rest (contraction) in between Her creative periods (expansion), revitalizing and refreshing Her being.

❖

Hence, the alchemically welded (fused) Life Energy and Life Force has become one, as Formed Life Being. And once welded, they can no longer return to their un-welded state. This is because the *essence of Life can never be destroyed once formed.* And even if it becomes deformed (such as the deforming of life in a bodily or mental sickness), it will not be permanent – for deformed Life can always be rescued, reformed and redeemed.

It is this Form Animating Life Principle "III" that deserts the mortal body and mind vehicles, rendering its form lifeless at death. This way the natural body/mind forms may return to the planetary body from which their forms originated – to help in the rebuilding of that planet's body and mind. (Detailed later.)

With the Third Stage of "Life Form," there is a THIRD stage of ETERNAL TIME manifested...for the Cosmic Mother understands that whenever anything is manifested, it must be sustained:

Four Steps toward the Manifesting of Eternal Time:

I Energy of Time: sustains Life Energy	II Force of Time: sustains Life Force
IV:III	III Form of Time: sustains Life Form

So with her Breath of Life, the Cosmic Mother's love and desire (heat) begins overflowing within the third part of Her being...

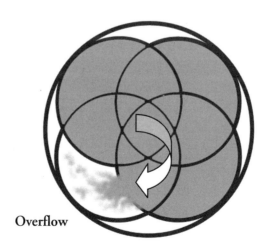

Overflow

*...Thus causing the Cosmic Mother to fully awaken from her sleep. This IGNITES the final aspect, her "SPACE-BEING" (3rd), bringing her from a conscious to a final **SELF-CONSCIOUS** and aware state... Enlightenment!*

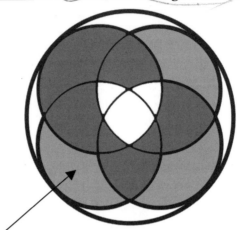

The self-conscious waking of the fourth aspect:
The "Space-Being" of God

With enlightenment, She is resplendent in all Her Glory — consumed by Her self-less desire to share Her love.

Willing to give up everything She is, for the new life within her womb, She exhales the Breath of Life — spreading its warmth like a blanket across all of space infinities. And with her own unlimited love selflessness (magnetic radiations), She causes a FOURTH Stage (quality) and step (quantity) toward the engendering of:

The Cosmic Trinity Creator (that will serve as Her spirit),
First Virgin Soul (as Her Soul) and
Creation (as Her body).

Life Form III absorbs the II and then the I, becoming:
*The Four Principle of... **Generation and Regeneration.***

IV

Love Principle

GENERATION

(Creation) and

REGENERATION

(Re-creation)

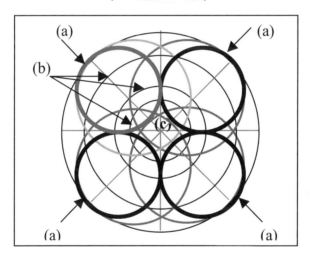

The fourth dimension comes to manifesting!

- *Symbolically, the Roman numeral "IV" stands for the Four or Love Principle, from which all has come. The "I" represents the Cosmic Mother and the V-shape (which cannot stand-alone), is the five of Life. Together, it reads, "the One that is Life bearing."*

- *The four circles (a), once entwined, now appear separate – representing the self-individualized being of the Trinity Creator and the First Virgin Soul. The three (lighter) rings in the center (b) represent life expanding outward from the womb, moving toward an independent living state. The very center (c) is the Soul core.*

165

With the 4th Step, the Cosmic Mother comes to
self-conscious waking and is enlightened from within…
endowed with the gift of great understanding,
The Wisdom of Love for all Life and all Living.

She becomes *Self*-consciously aware, that it was Her own SELF-LESS *BEING*, sustaining Her consciousness as She slept. It was SHE, who both GAVE and SUSTAINED HER OWN LIFE! It was SHE WHO GAVE HER OWN BREATH…THAT GAVE HER BEING! She comes to the enlightened understanding that…

SHE IS LIFE! Glorious Life! Her own self-less, sustainable
BEING   IS   LIFE,   Ever-living…Ever-breathing…BEING,
CONTAINING   and   SUSTAINING   ALL   THAT
EXISTS…OUT OF LOVE.
She is the CAUSAL MOTHER ever-sharing Herself for
GOD IS LIFE, whose nature is LOVE!

Her *Self's* consciousness realized who and what She was, *"As above, so below"* – She too goes through self-realization and Enlightenment. She understands that…

She shall sustain and contain all that shall come forth from Her.
And that She shall give Her Life and Light to ignite the
Consciousness of all Creation. With this igniting will come the
understanding that: Consciousness is transformed by Love the
Wisdom of Love for all Life and all living. And through this
understanding (standing under the Light) ALL is made purified
to return to Her as One.

This is a glorious moment! Because the Four Principle of "Generation and Regeneration" (on a chemical/cellular and alchemical level/love) *allows* for the first division of the masculine and feminine as living, propagating states:

> *With the movement of individualized Life within Her womb,
> there is the first division…She bursts forth in resplendent glory as
> the heat of love rises from within Her being.*

> *Welled with anticipation, She tears away the veil of the
> unknown – And is brought to ecstasy! Behold, from within
> Her…the first living Life and Light body…**the Cosmic Trinity
> Creator!** She is now, not only Life bearing, but also Light or
> Truth bearing. For **Light is Truth…a living thing!** The
> Trinity Creator Himself will carry the Light or Truth to be
> transmitted to his creations and mankind!*

> *Oh, how She had dreamed of You and now you are here. Her
> dream has become a reality…She is **Dreaming True!** The
> Cosmic Mother shares Her love with the infant – thus from her
> eternal essence He shall soon be born.*

So God said, "Let there be light…"

> *And with that, Love's fire ignites the consciousness of the
> Trinity Creator into a three-in-one state of living
> consciousness, lovingly contained and sustained by and from
> within Her womb.*

Now, the veil is drawn open and she can see:

> *The Cosmic Mother envisions the remaining five steps that will
> bring Her generation to birth, along with the (feminine) Virgin
> Soul and Creation.*

But alas, there is something else…

The Cosmic Mother realizes that with the Fourth stage of the manifesting of a new life, She has also experienced the *final* Fourth stage of Eternal Time manifesting. This means that Eternal Time is ready to be brought to birth:

Four Steps toward the Manifesting of Eternal Time:	
I Energy of Time: sustains Life Energy	II Force of Time: sustains Life Force
IV:III Generation & Regeneration Faculty of Time	III Form of Time: sustains Life Form

This Eternal Time substance, up till now, had been sustaining the Cosmic Trinity Creator *within* Her inner space, Her womb. But once the Trinity Creator is born, She needs that time substance to sustain the Trinity Creator, Creation, and all of nature occupying the space *outside Her womb:*

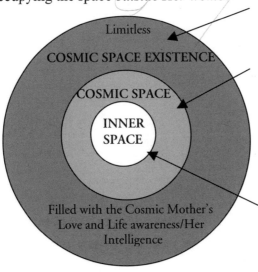

Future home of Creation: where we will live and breathe and have being

Cosmic space: the nursery to be occupied by the Trinity Creator, Virgin Soul Nature, and Creation...the Cosmic Mother's home environment

Womb: Trinity Creator, Virgin Soul Nature, and Creation being sustained by Eternal Time

*From the beginning, Eternal Time lay within the Cosmic Mother's womb helping to sustain the generation to be conceived. But now, her faithful servant Chimaera, ETERNAL TIME, is fully formed, fully endowed and ready to be brought to birth as (two-fold) **ETERNITY & TIME!***

*Behold, Eternity & Time will come forth in the next step, before the Trinity Creator, Virgin Soul Nature and Creation is born, to prepare the nursery – recondition the space – **outside** the Cosmic Mother's womb.*

*Once born, ETERNITY...shall reign within the **upper**, spirit life and heavenly regions of space, sustaining the environment and giving infinite love and Life (duration) to all that reside there.*

*And TIME...shall fill the form regions **below**, where **we** will eventually live and breathe and have **our** being. Time will impart a natural termination (death), to any physical form manifest in time and will ultimately become the servant of the Trinity Creator.*

*The Cosmic Mother must now give the Trinity Creator, Virgin Soul Nature, and Creation, **individualized Life.** And to do this She must again **recreate Her own** for **SHE IS LIFE... ALL OF LIFE** and must give up ALL She is and ALL She has, to make Her Generation a self-breathing, living state!*

Even knowing that…

*Once She gives all She is and all She has, **She shall create no more** (until the end of the cycle) – for She will have given away all three masculine aspects of Her being, along with all Her **creative ability.** **Thus,** after the birth of the Trinity Creator (the Big Bang), She becomes CREATIVELY EXHAUSTED, for the One can only divide itself by itself! **Only once:***

I = 1/1 lesser units in the image of Unity.

**The Cosmic Mother with
four aspects to Her being**

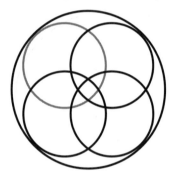

SHE FIRST DIVIDES WITHIN HER WOMB:

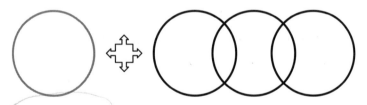

*Redemptive/Recreative
(Motivated by Love)*
Feminine

*Creative
(Lays Potent – Motivated by
pressure to create/expands)*
Masculine

170

By giving the Trinity individualized Life, the Cosmic Mother will redeem, recreate, and sacrifice her own. And She will give herself with no regret – for although She will create no more, the Trinity will remember her dreams; and once He is born, will make them a reality.

*And as the Trinity creates **ALL LIVING and CREATION**, the Cosmic Mother will lovingly sustain it. **Because ALL** – anything and everything that exists – IS HER, and is being SUSTAINED and CONTAINED BY HER LIFE and LIGHT of intelligence.*

She gives this out of love, and Her Sons in understanding this, will love, cherish and protect all Life and all Living, imbued by their Mother's being, the Source from which they have come...

> The Tao is infinite, eternal.
> Why is it eternal?
> It was never born;
> Thus it can never die.
> Why is it infinite?
> It has no desires for itself;
> Thus it is present for all beings.
> Tao Te Ching

*And again, with the heat of the Cosmic Mother's love and Life understanding, along with Her Breath of Life, She **contracts, causing a FIFTH Stage and step** toward the engendering of: the Cosmic Trinity Creator (who will later serve as Her spirit), first Virgin Soul (who will later serve as Her Soul) and Creation (which will later serve as Her body).*

*Generation and Regeneration IV absorb the III, II and I (in reverse order), becoming: The Five Principle of **LIFE!***

The Five of Life

V

LIFE

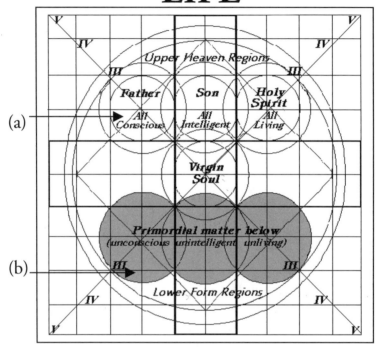

- The "V" shape form of the Roman Numeral Five, symbolizes a funneling of Life into the form worlds below. The shape itself cannot stand-alone, so we see the V sustained by the Love or "I" in the IV principle, or sustained by the "I" in the "VI" principle, which is a self-individualized state of living.

- The light (a) and dark circles (b) represent Space going through a contraction, and differentiation of space – light circles (a) in the Heaven regions and darker circles (b) in the Time regions below. The three circles above have been bestowed upon them: All Conscious, All Intelligence and All Living; leaving unconscious, unintelligent, un-living primordial matter in the three darker circles in the Time regions below.

172

The Infant Trinity Creator is given the essence of Life And the 5ᵗʰ dimension comes into being...

In the Fifth Step, a series of wondrous events take place *simultaneously:*

a) We see the origin of primordial matter.

b) The Cosmic Mother selflessly give up her **Spiritmind**, that will carry **all** her consciousness, intelligence, and living to the Trinity Creator.

c) There is the birth of Eternal Time. And;

d) The differentiating of space: space divides into two regions.

With all Her love (heat) and selfless desire...

The Cosmic Mother begins to **creatively CONTRACT.** *The heat is so concentrated and with such great intensity and pressure that Space curdles – moving, stretching – causing a* **spiritmind substance*** *to be formed...*

As the Cosmic Mother contracts, a spiritmind substance* is formed. This substance will carry **ALL** of the Cosmic Mother's consciousness, intelligence, and living to the "infant" within Her womb. And once absorbed by the Trinity, it will leave everything else *mindless*...hence, we find the origin of *primordial matter*...along with the origins of *passion* and *compassion:*

So overwhelmed was She by her **PASSION** *to give birth to the Trinity Creator, that in that moment* **She contracts, taking up**

---

* spiritmind substance: a rarified (etherialized) densification known as her Spiritmind, which carries the conscious intelligence of the Cosmic Mother's "self."

*ALL her CONSCIOUSNESS throughout ALL her being, and makes the infant Trinity Creator **ALL-CONSCIOUS** within Her womb. Thus, leaving the **UNCONSCIOUS** aspect of primordial matter in the densified Time regions below.*

*And upon seeing this **UN-CONSCIOUS** emptiness in the densified regions below, She felt its hunger and yearning to become conscious again…*

*So moved is She by Her **COMPASSION** for this unconscious emptiness, that She simultaneously fills this void and sustains it with the (one-dimensional) **Energy** aspect of Time. This in turn, becomes the **first** **UNCONSCIOUS** **energy aspect of Primordial Matter,** (first of four stages) the origins of the future building block of nature:*

Trinity Creator is made…

ALL-CONSCIOUS

Leaving an Unconscious aspect of Primordial Matter below (now filled and sustained by the **Energy 1** aspect of Time).

Unconscious Primordial Matter: which the Trinity Creator shall create with after his birth.

---

*Then again with all Her **PASSION**, She **contracts,** this time taking up ALL Her **INTELLIGENCE** throughout ALL Her being, and makes the infant Trinity Creator **ALL-INTELLIGENT** within her womb. Thus leaving the*

UNINTELLIGENT aspect of primordial matter in the densified Time regions below.

*And upon seeing this **UNINTELLIGENT** emptiness with its hunger for that which was taken away, She simultaneously fills this void and sustains it with the (two-dimensional) **Force** aspect of Time. This in turn, becomes the **second UNINTLLIGENT** aspect of Primordial Matter (second of four stages towards the manifesting of matter in the Time regions below):*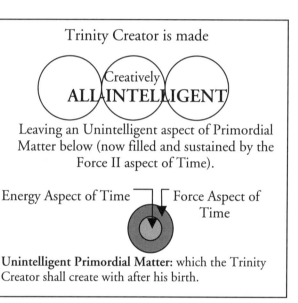

Trinity Creator is made

Creatively
ALL-INTELLIGENT

Leaving an Unintelligent aspect of Primordial Matter below (now filled and sustained by the Force II aspect of Time).

Energy Aspect of Time ⌐ ⌐ Force Aspect of Time

Unintelligent Primordial Matter: which the Trinity Creator shall create with after his birth.

*And then again, in self-less love for the infant within Her womb, She **contracts**, taking up **ALL** Her **LIVING** throughout **ALL** Her being, making the Trinity Creator **ALL-LIVING** within Her ...Leaving the **UNLIVING** aspect of primordial matter in the densified Time regions below.*

*And as She gazes upon this **UNLIVING** emptiness, with its hunger for Life, She can bare the pain no more. Through Her compassion, She fills and sustains it – but this time by the Form* *aspect of Time – which becomes the **third** or UNLIVING aspect of Primordial Matter:*

Trinity Creator is made

Leaving an Unliving aspect of **Primordial Matter** below (now filled and sustained by the Form III aspect of Time).

1)Energy Aspect of Time   2)Force Aspect of Time
3) Form Aspect of Time

Unliving Primordial Matter: which the Trinity Creator shall create with after his birth.

Though all three aspects of the Trinity Creator are made All-conscious, All-intelligent and All-living...

All Her consciousness is emphasized in the Father aspect,
All Her intelligence is emphasized in the Son aspect,
All Her living is emphasized in the Holy Spirit aspect.

In the Time regions, where primordial matter has begun to manifest…

The three-dimensional unconscious, unintelligent and unliving primordial matter stood frozen – imprisoned within their three dimensions of form…

Matter was imprisoned within its own form, because:

a) The entire first dimension is filled with unconsciousness, sustained by the energy aspect of Time substance.

b) The entire second dimension is filled with unintelligence, sustained by the force aspect of Time substance.

c) The entire third dimension is filled with the unliving, sustained by the form aspect of Time substance.

Since a three-dimensional form completely fills all three dimensions of its space, it has no more space in which to move:

Thus there came the Fourth, Generation aspect of Time…It surrounds the three-dimensional primordial matter, permeating all aspects of its dense form – filling it with the fourth dimension! And the primordial matter, which once stood frozen in three dimensions of space, was now set free…moving through its Four-dimensional space!

One more dimension was added to the three, allowing it the space in which to move: (Sec illustration)

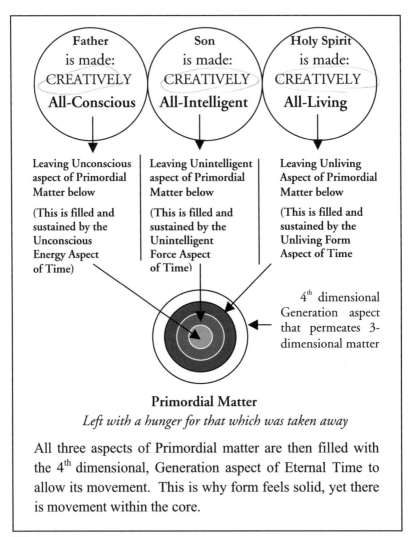

Father is made: CREATIVELY All-Conscious	Son is made: CREATIVELY All-Intelligent	Holy Spirit is made: CREATIVELY All-Living
Leaving Unconscious aspect of Primordial Matter below	Leaving Unintelligent aspect of Primordial Matter below	Leaving Unliving Aspect of Primordial Matter below
(This is filled and sustained by the Unconscious Energy Aspect of Time)	(This is filled and sustained by the Unintelligent Force Aspect of Time)	(This is filled and sustained by the Unliving Form Aspect of Time)

4th dimensional Generation aspect that permeates 3-dimensional matter

Primordial Matter
Left with a hunger for that which was taken away

All three aspects of Primordial matter are then filled with the 4th dimensional, Generation aspect of Eternal Time to allow its movement. This is why form feels solid, yet there is movement within the core.

Note:

As the Cosmic Mother **contracts,** Space the container of Her being is *differentiated into different regions.* This differentiating (re-conditioning or reshaping) of space is what Marie called, "Creative-Created Polarization." Her **creative** aspects (consciousness, intelligence, and living) are sent above where the region has become a four-dimensional rarified (refined) state. Simultaneously, the environment in the lower **created** regions, left with primordial matter, becomes a four-dimensional densified (dense) state. Here is where anything created will soon exist. This is similar to Hyperspace theory, where space splits between the fourth and sixth-dimension.

Thus with Her contraction:

*Space, the container of Her being, was then divided, differentiated, and thereby transformed into the **future nursery** in preparation for the Generation within Her womb.*

*The **upper** regions of Space were gloriously filled with Love, Life, and Light! This **Heaven**...would become the future home of the **"creative"** Trinity Creator.*

*The **lower** regions were left dark, lifeless, and without love, with a hunger to be filled again. This "Time" region, within space-existence, would later become the future home of all "**created**" creation: i.e., earth, planets, and nature.*

*However, where the upper and lower regions crossed (or overlapped in the **center**), there became the **Central Soul Regions** – And it would be here, where our future Souls would await to be **quickened** and Divinely sent to birth!*

The following drawing shows the differentiating of the Cosmic Mother's home environment. The *creative* aspects lying above, while the *created* aspects lie below: (See illustration next page.)

The Differentiation of Space:

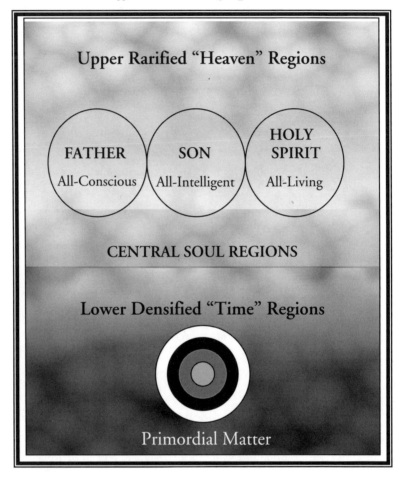

Upper Rarified "Heaven" Regions

FATHER
All-Conscious

SON
All-Intelligent

HOLY SPIRIT
All-Living

CENTRAL SOUL REGIONS

Lower Densified "Time" Regions

Primordial Matter

Note: Since 3/4 of primordial matter is contained within the third-dimension, and 1/4 of it is in the fourth-dimension, it becomes logical that all movement of forms, including perpetual motion of Time's past into future, occurs in the fourth dimension.

This is why we cannot see the past or future – it is in perpetual motion – anything in motion occurs within the fourth dimension. Our three-dimensional human form isn't equipped to see into the fourth dimension...unless it has been conditioned.

And finally, with the Fifth Step – as space differentiates…

> *The Cosmic Mother's servant, Eternal Time, is born. Eternal Time is born as dually manifested, **Eternity and Time**.*
>
> *That portion of Eternal Time that manifests in the upper space regions (to be occupied by the Infant Trinity Creator) becomes **Eternity**. Eternity will sustain and fill all of the Heaven regions of Space, imparting a sense of Ever-Living to all Spirit and forms that shall occupy it.*
>
> *And that portion of Eternal Time that occupies the deserted and deprived densified form regions (occupied by three-dimensional primordial matter) manifests as **Time**.[19] And it shall sustain and fill all of the lower regions of space, imparting a **sense** of life-time termination (death), which leads us to believe that one lifetime is all we will have…*
>
> *Eternity and Time will never be divided, for in the center, where one overlaps the other, there lies the Central Soul Region – A purely fourth-dimensional extension, occupied by the first and future, infant Virgin Soul: (See illustration on the following page.)*
>
> *And though we may feel sorrow for Creation, sent to live among the limited regions of Time, we must trust and believe that ALL shall be redeemed – for She has sent us Time that will sustain us. It shall sustain Humanity and creation long enough that **we** may be redeemed, recreated, and received in Love…thereby furthering our journey, to return to Her as One.*

---

[19] Later, time will consume the third dimension, so it may time the amount of energy that goes into the matter.

ETERNITY
Heaven Region...
Where the Cosmic Mother dwells
To be occupied by the Trinity Creator

Four-dimensional rarified, and
Three-dimensional
rarified space

SPIRIT-LIFE REGION

CENTRAL SOUL REGION
This region is later redeemed and immortalized by
the occupancy of the first, Infant Virgin Soul Nature
Purely fourth-dimensional – Diffused

(This region is diffused, because there is no third-dimension
within it...only Fourth-dimensional Eternity and Fourth-
dimensional aspect of Time overlapping one another)

TIME
Created Natural Region...
Primordial Matter and later form worlds

Four-dimensionally densified – Anti-polar
– Three-dimensional densified space

Creatively Deprived

The Cosmic Mother has made a great sacrifice in relinquishing the three *masculine and conscious* aspects of Her being to the infant Trinity Creator, along with ALL Her ability to create. And though He may share these creative abilities with all of Creation:

> ***"Laws and ways of Creation are great*** Redemption
> ***but laws and ways of Redemption*** ✓
> ***are greater...***
> Sir Francis Bacon's, *Advancement of Learning*

The "III" quality of Trinity Creator is great, but the "IV" or Love Principle of the Causal Redemptive Virgin Mother is greater, because She is the Cause of Life... the Mystery of the Four is revealed.

> ***Life determined laws and ways of Creation or Generation***
> ***are inseparable from love-determined laws and ways of***
> ***re-creation or regeneration."***
> *Marie Bauer Hall*

The laws of Creation (*Creative III Principle*) used by the Trinity Creator cannot be separated from the laws and love of the (IV or Love Principle) Cosmic Mother.

The chemical and alchemical "V" of Life ingredients has now been welded into the Fifth State of Life and cannot go back to their pre-welded, individual state of Life ingredients. This is why you cannot destroy Life...however it can be **deformed.** We see this deforming in death and sickness, whereby this newly created Life is not being warmth or love-sustained. Without this warmth or love, Life becomes deformed. However, with proper enlightened understanding, Life can be reformed yet again.

God As Mother

The essence of **Life** is a Being,
Life is God!
The essence of God is **being**
Therefore, our being is **God.**

With space now *re-conditioned,* it brings us to the next
step in the engendering of the infant Trinity Creator, infant Virgin
Soul Nature and infant Creation:

*With the Cosmic Mother's enlightened Love and Life
understanding, along with Her **Breath of Life,** She causes a
SIXTH Stage or Step toward the engendering of:*

*The Cosmic Trinity Creator (that will serve as Her spirit)
First Virgin Soul (as Her Soul) and Creation (as Her body)…
And through a chemical and alchemical process (love) the Five of
Life, V, absorbs the IV, III, II and then the I, welding them
together, becoming: The Six Principle of **LIVING!***

VI
LIVING

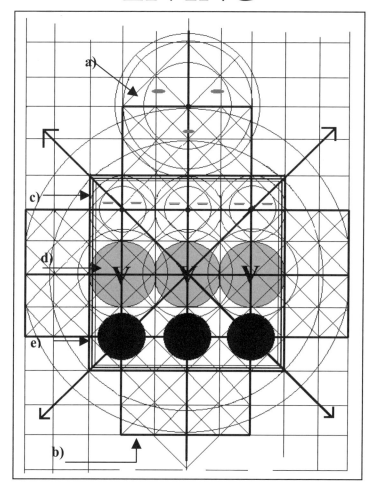

The Sixth Dimension comes to manifesting!

- The circle on top (a) represents the Cosmic Mother.
- The wide, darkened cross at center (b) represents Her Love and Life expanding outward, as each step is taken toward the Trinity's manifesting.

- The upper three circles (c) with faces represent the Trinity's newly formed triple, self-individualized state.
- The three central circles (d) with the "V" or Five of Life, represent their newly forming Virgin Souls – that will sustain them once they leave the womb.
- The black circles are the result of the Cosmic Mother endowing the Trinity with all Her consciousness, intelligence and living, leaving the unconscious, unintelligent, and unliving emptiness in the black circles (e) below.
- The squares, including the darker, triple-lined square at center, represent the mind, as the Trinity Creator absorbs it within each step.
- The diamond shapes within the squares represent "awareness," as a living state moves (expands) through it.

With the SIXTH STEP, the infant, masculine, Trinity Creator becomes a Living self-breathing, (three-in-one) state of being...
The first state of self-individualized living!

In the Fourth Step, the infant, Trinity Creator becomes a *living consciousness* (though not yet breathing on its own, and still dependent upon the Cosmic Mother). In the Fifth Step the Trinity Creator is given the essence of Life and intelligence. With the Sixth Step, the Trinity becomes a living self-breathing state:

The wondrous flames of Love dwelling within Her being, swelled to ignite the Life within Her womb.
*And at that moment, the three **Selfhoods** *of the Cosmic Mother are transformed, becoming a complete living, **self-breathing** state...able to live on, beyond Her womb...a true "Living" state of consciousness.*

---

* selfhoods: plural of "self" (three-in-one).

The three-in-one Spiritself of the Father, Son, and Holy Spirit, is the first **Self** that is individualized. Though a trinity, each now has a mind and a creative consciousness of their own.

And as life moved within the Cosmic Mother's womb, She rejoiced – for there also lies the first purely feminine, Cosmic Virgin Soul...

It is a pure, virgin state – Virgin meaning "selfless" –
no ego or *"self"* within it.

Though the Cosmic Mother has four aspects to her nature, the Trinity (three white areas) only absorbs three of her magnetic parts (a) (gray areas). This leaves one whole magnetic part (b) left unattached to any Spiritself of the Trinity:

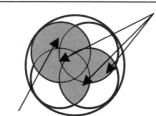

a) **Magnetic overflow (gray) sustaining the three Spiritselves (in white) of the Trinity Creator**

b) **Selfless Causal Being, the Soul Core - with no Spiritself attached. A purely magnetic love-warmth.**

1) The magnetic **overflow** (a) (gray) from the Soul Core of the Cosmic Mother (b), becomes the Virgin Souls for each of the Trinity's selves (white).

2) But the fourth (b) remains **Selfless** (no Spiritself attached)...This **Soul Core**, will become the future Cosmic Egg, from which many Souls will be born.

Within the Soul Core, lies the selfless Virgin Soul Nature[*] that will not only communicate with all other Souls it engenders, but it **will be the only aspect that stays directly connected to the Cosmic Mother:**

> *This Virgin Soul has a Soulmind that uses awareness as its intelligence. And it is the Cosmic Mother's unlimited Love-Awareness that sustains all Life and light or living intelligence...*

Awareness & Consciousness

While the Soul has a Soulmind that uses **awareness**, the Spiritself ("self" of the Trinity Creator's spirit), has a spiritmind that uses **consciousness** for its intelligence. However this consciousness is **limited**, and must be sustained by the awareness of the Soul. (An example of its limitations is when our light of consciousness goes out, during sleep – to replenish itself. However, we are sustained by the awareness of the Soul.)

Awareness: is the *Light and Life-sustaining* factor of intelligence.

Consciousness: Is the light factor that *lights up* intelligence.

For example: Awareness is the hydro-electric system within a dam that creates and sustains the electricity. Consciousness is the newly formed electricity, lighting up the bulb or intelligence).

---

[*] Virgin Soul Nature: is not yet occupied by a Spiritself, hence its virgin "Nature."

Here is a chart comparing the Awareness of the Soul, with the limitations of consciousness or intelligence of the self:

AWARENESS VS CONSCIOUSNESS

AWARENESS OF THE SOUL (Flows through the Soulmind)	CONSCIOUSNESS OF THE SELF (Flows through the Spiritmind)
Awareness is a LOVE intelligence.	Consciousness is CREATIVE intelligence (creative consciousness).
The NATURE of Awareness is LOVE.	The NATURE of Consciousness is light. Consciousness is transformed and made purified by LOVE (heat).
Awareness is "SELFLESS" - without self, therefore LOVE-CENTERED. (Works through love.)	Consciousness is "SELF"-CENTERED.
Awareness is selfless therefore expresses itself in selfless and self-humbled service (self-forgetful).	Consciousness is self-serving, self-displaying, and self-expressing.
Awareness is LIMITLESS – Because the Soul is "selfless," without self, it's intelligence is "limitless." It is the self that places limitations upon us. Being limitless, makes the awareness of the Soul, Eternal, Ever-living, ever breathing, Life and Light sustaining and replenishing. RECREATES and Redeems Life and living intelligence. *	Consciousness is LIMITED – Because the "self" restrains and confines creating boundaries to impose reason, its consciousness is limited. It is also self-expending, using up its Life and Light – therefore it becomes DEATH-CREATIVE perishable unless it is replenished and sustained by the Soul. (Consciousness is Virgin Love-formed and so must be warmth or love-sustained.)

Awareness of the Soul (cont'd)	Consciousness of the Self (cont'd)
Awareness is UNLIMITED - ALWAYS AWAKE. Sustains life and light.	Consciousness is LIMITED – ALTERNATES between a conscious through unconscious state. Goes to an unconscious state (as in sleep) to replenish its life and light.
Awareness uses the Soulmind (mind of the Soul) to UNITE our thoughts and experiences becoming "understanding." Awareness encompasses Universal mind and thought using multi-dimensional thinking.	Consciousness uses the natural mind (physical) and spiritmind (of self) to CHOPS THINGS UP and BREAK THINGS DOWN to become "knowledge" – It uses trial and error thinking along with its natural reason to separate into parts so that it may be known.
The Soul's Awareness uses SPIRITUAL REASON to access and absorb UNDERSTANDING.	The self's consciousness uses CREATIVE REASON to access and absorb knowledge so that is may become KNOWN. (You can know more than you understand.)
The Soul's Awareness is accessed and influenced by emotional means (i.e. feeling, spiritual intuition) Uses spiritual reason via "New Dimensional Thinking."	The self's consciousness is accessed and influenced by rational means. Uses creative reason via trial and error thinking.
Awareness is "Being," that sustains intelligence; It is being awake and at One. It is a unifying, NOW experience. Timeless.	Consciousness is light, the pathway of intelligence. Varies or fluctuates between conscious/self-conscious/ subconscious, and unconscious states. Consciousness chops time up, dividing our experiences between the past and future.

Awareness of the Soul (cont'd)	Consciousness of the Self (cont'd)
Awareness is "redemptive" wisdom that can be livingly or parentally transmitted – exempt from death.	Creative wisdom is form bound and time perpetuated within art and writing, which makes it perishable, subject to death or extinction.
Through the use of Awareness we can experience INITIATION from WITHIN. This is called "re-creatively (sacrificed) conscious wisdom attainment" – the true "Wisdom of Love for All Life and All Living." It is "experienced distilled understanding," which is accessed through a personal experience that has been absorbed and understood from within; or expressed in active endeavor or service toward the betterment of mankind. It is "Redemptive" (motivated by love).	Through the use of Consciousness we can experience INITIATION from WITHOUT. This is called "creatively conscious wisdom attainment." This can make you receptive to enlightenment, PREPARES YOU, but it cannot cause you to be enlightened. Creative conscious knowing or wisdom is gathered by the natural mind from without. (Not personally experienced.)[20]
Awareness is called the "re-creative awareness."	Consciousness is called the Creative-consciousness.
Awareness is of original expression: synthesis.	Creative-Consciousness is of imitative expression: division.
Awareness (pre big-bang) is dark Love warmth...the mother of light.	Consciousness (pre big-bang) is dark or dormant light.
Awareness unites and sustains aspects of a relationship.	Consciousness divides aspects of a relationship.

[20] This can be re-influenced through audio visual means. See *New Dimensional Thinking*, Jennings.

Awareness of the Soul (cont'd)	Consciousness of the Self (cont'd)
A Virgin Soul reaction causes experienced distilled understanding and living waking for the building of Virgin Soul minds.	Limited mind formed, human trial and error thinking and *knowing* must be transformed into Virgin Soul *understanding*. (It's the creative consciousness that's doing all the questioning. Mind is the substance that carries the creative consciousness. Like a vital etheric transparent-like glass or mirror. The black stuff on the back of the mirror is the brain.*)

❖

Ending of the Sixth Step:

So, with the Cosmic Mother's enlightened Love and Life understanding, She reinforces the heat of Her Love with Her Breath of Life and causes a SEVENTH Stage or Step toward the engendering of...

The Cosmic Trinity Creator (as Her spirit),
First Virgin Soul (as Her Soul) and
Creation (as Her body).

And through a chemical and alchemical process (love), the Six of Living "VI" absorbs the V, IV, III, II and I, in reverse order. The Cosmic Mother then reinforces the heat of Her Love with the Breath of Life, causing the next step of: The Seven Principle of *EVER-LIVING!*

---

* See: *New Dimensional Thinking*, V. Jennings

EVER-LIVING
VII

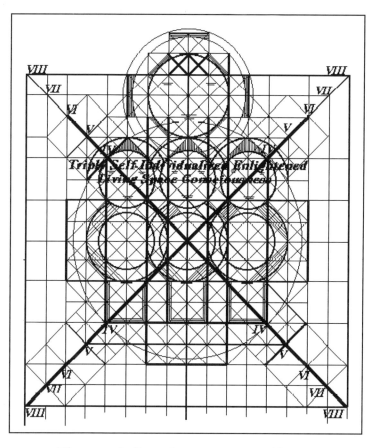

The seventh dimension comes to manifesting!

With the SEVENTH STEP, the Cosmic Mother endows the infant Trinity Creator with the gift of Her "EVER-living...Eternal Life," which can subsequently be shared with all of His creations to come!

193

With Eternal Life, the Trinity is endowed with insight into the Love Mysteries – the Cosmic Mother's mysterious and divine relationship to all Creation. He is also endowed with Life and death understanding of the perishability of Life – for anything He creates, cannot alone sustain itself, without her love-warmth. And lastly, He understands the process of perfecting life: through Birth, Death, and Resurrection – as the Way to return to the One.

*The Trinity will in turn, impart this **Divine Understanding** to all that He creates…maintaining the connection to the Source by instilling the memory of the Causal Virgin Mother into the Soulminds of all His creations.*

Review: In Step Five, the infant Trinity Creator receives the **mind substance** that carries the (all-conscious, all intelligent, and all living) *spiritmind* of the Cosmic Mother. In Step Six, He is self-individualized and can live beyond her womb.

However in Step Seven, the Cosmic Mother causes the *welding* of the Trinity Creator's Spiritself with their spiritmind:

*With the welding of the Trinity's Spiritself and spiritmind, the first **creative self-consciousness** is born. This creative-consciousness, allows the Trinity to communicate and share in the rapture of the Cosmic Mother's Love and Light of Wisdom.*

From the moment the Trinity is born, this spiritmind shall serve as a vehicle that will carry his creative-consciousness along with the Trinity's newly formed concepts and ideas.

*This spiritmind substance will then be worked by the Trinity's consciousness, into His **mind faculties** – with which He will build the works of creation.*

The Arcanum

These mind faculties will be differentiated as:

- ***Spiritual Memory** – so He may remember from where He has come*

- ***Spiritual Imagination** – so He may dream of things not yet seen*

- ***Spiritual Reason** – to understand the true, underlying principles of creation and how they unfold*

- ***Creative Projection** – the ability to manifest that which is seen*

- ***Freewill** – to determine his fate: as to how and when He comes to be enlightened and...*

- ***Spiritual Intuition** – so He may always stay connected to Her... as One!*

*These **mind faculties** are the tools the Trinity will use to create His Cosmic Mother's dreams of form evolution and spirit involution – envisioning, refining, and committing these ideas to reality.*

*And after the Trinity is born, He will use his spiritmind to experience the joys of creative expression, communication, and self-conscious **mind purification**.*

Mind purification is the maturing, evolving and transforming of the Trinity Creator's mind, as His consciousness matures. By going through this process of purifying (re-creating)

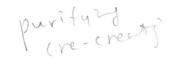

the mind, He too will reach enlightened understanding whereby his origin, purpose, and destiny are revealed…"As above, so below."

The Three Minds of Man

Man, being a composite human, has three different bodies: a physical body, spiritbody and Soulbody. And each body has a mind: the Soul has a Soulmind, the Spirit has a spiritmind, and the physical body has a natural mind. Each mind has its own mind faculties (memory, reason, imagination, creative projection, freewill, intuition) that are being used in different ways. Here are a few examples:

Memory

On a physical level, we use the *natural mind,* which is supported by the brain. The natural mind contains the memories of every day life: *natural memories* consisting of fleeting events, thoughts, and deeds. Because the physical form stores these natural memories in the brain, they affect us on a physical level. We see its effect as illness, attributed to memories that trigger emotions that further trigger corresponding physical reactions. Since natural memories are absorbed by form, they are as temporary as the physical form itself…and will either dissipate or be absorbed into its evolutionary, natural order. At death, the physical body along with its natural memories is returned to the very make-up of the **body and mind** of the earth from which it had come. This process either regenerates or degenerates the Earth…depending on the purity of the Soul residing within that physical body and mind.

On a Spirit level we use our spiritmind with its *spiritual memory* containing information held from lifetime to lifetime. These spiritual memories consist of life changing events, thoughts, and deeds that are experienced on a chemical and alchemical level. On a chemical level, these essences are purified. On an alchemical level, they are distilled into essences that are built into the Soul. However if an individual lives an *inauthentic* life, perverting the life experience, then these distilled essences of the spiritual memories will go to reinforcing of the self (ego) rather than the Soul. Hence, the Soul is deprived of vital essences, retarding its growth.

On a Soul level we use our Soulmind with its **Soul memory** containing information held since before the beginning of time. Its memories are eternal, timeless; its language is a code – a *pattern* within which one may remember the experience of true Oneness...it is the *Mind of God* itself. Its essences are pure, sustained by the warmth of God's Life and Love. We access it through a state of awareness, the life and light-sustaining factor of intelligence.

Imagination

Another brief example is our use of imagination and reason. In our daily lives we use our natural imagination to project the practical details of everyday life. But it is from within our ***spiritual imagination*** that we may catch glimpses of the Divine, envisioning the great gifts to humanity, and the perfecting of our art.

Reason

By seeking to define the principles and laws of God and creation through the use of our faculty of ***spiritual reason,*** an entirely new landscape of invisible worlds can be opened before our eyes. We are no longer limited to the three-dimensional universe of creative reason. Instead, through spiritual reason, we have the capacity to access and assimilate the knowledge of infinite worlds of origins and causes in a multi-dimensional universe.

It is with our spiritual reason, with its unlimited scope, that we can conceive of the nature of God, in terms of the infinite, timeless, and omnipresent. It places information accumulated from lifetimes of experiences into a higher order of "alignment"...as one. And once aligned, experienced as "understanding," the self-centered "self" can be absorbed into the "selfless" love-centered nature of the Soul.

These were just a few examples of the mind faculties lying within us, and for many, will lie dormant and unused. Our task in this lifetime is to reactivate them...through the development of a love-awareness of Life and living...by a wakefulness sustained in the now, standing on the bridge between the past and our future.[*]

❖

Next, with love and great understanding, the Cosmic Mother bestows the infant within Her womb, with the power of Freewill!

Freewill is given to allow the infant Trinity Creator to choose his own path, in his own time, by his own means – as to how He will come to a greater understanding of his Love and Life Destiny.

His Freewill determines the course He will take in his own transformation – for the very choices He makes influence his ability to self-recreate: the distilling, and purifying of his own conscious self and being.

---

[*] See New Dimensional Thinking for in-depth study.

Freewill, Fate & Destiny

Freewill = choices   Fate = process   Destiny = outcome

Freewill governs the choices that we make, and these choices will govern our fate. *Fate is the process*...the different experiences that purify us and will ultimately lead us to our destiny. *Destiny is the outcome,* and your destiny, my destiny, everyone's destiny, is the same – to return to the Source as One.

Because Life has an innate need to evolve, Man's destiny cannot be changed – his evolution is innate. And if through his freewill he makes a choice that **does not** support his evolution, or cause experiences that move him toward his destiny, fate steps in – temporarily taking away his freewill – and readjusts the path. When this happens, fate becomes an invisible, yet powerfully innate force that influences lifetimes of our natural unfolding and evolution of being. Fate will create the necessary experiences – intelligent, intricate patterns, web-like paths – drawing people or circumstances that *will* lead one back to their destiny.

Dr. Micheal Barnsley, chief scientist of Iterated Systems Inc., stated:

> "God has created a system which gave us freewill...the most brilliant maneuver in the Universe, to create something in which everything is free...how could you do that?"

This idea of the relationship between freewill, fate, and destiny, supports two ideas: physicist Max Born's theory that "God plays dice"; and Einstein's theory of order, "deterministic laws."

I believe that this Divine Order or Universal Law of Einstein exists within the nature or essence of a creation – the law

199

being, that it continually evolves – by replicating or mirroring the very perfection of the "Life" (pattern) within. This makes it "deterministic" in principle. However, the various paths of its evolution are determined by freewill, and here's where we see that God plays dice. There are infinite ways through which we may choose to evolve. And in moving from one scale to another, God being infinite, wouldn't its creation be infinite?

But the power of freewill is not held for long. As the infant Trinity Creator goes through infancy, childhood, adolescence, and Cosmic Soul maturing, He shall gain the understanding of his origins, purpose, and destiny. And with this understanding...He is transformed.

*Through this process of Transformation, and Enlightenment, He will slowly "relinquish" his freewill, so that He may live by **Her** laws,...moving from separateness to Oneness. Hence, "Thy will be done..."*

We are now brought to the next step...

With the Cosmic Mother's enlightened Love and Life understanding, along with Her Breath of Life, She causes an EIGHTH Stage and Step toward the engendering of...

The Cosmic Trinity Creator (as Her spirit)
First Virgin Soul (as Her Soul) and
Creation (as Her body)

*And through a chemical and alchemical process (Her Love), the Seven of Ever-Living absorbs the VI, V, IV, III, II and the I, in reverse order, welding them together, and becoming: The Eight Principle of **EVER-LOVING!***

VIII
EVER-LOVING

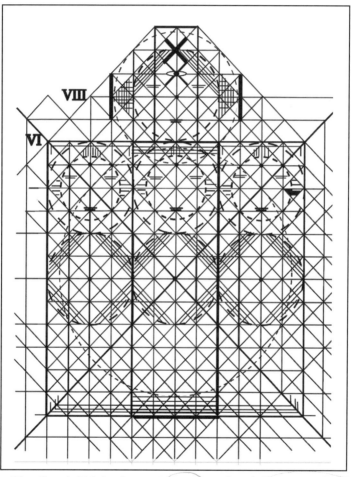

- The Cosmic Trinity Creator is Love-manifested, Love-engendered, Love-enlightened, Love-contained and Love-sustained.

The eighth dimension comes to manifesting!

In the EIGHTH Step…

> *The Cosmic Mother telepathically projects*
> *Her Love Nature to the infant Trinity Creator,*
> *endowing Him with the gift of Her "Ever-Loving,"*
> *so that Love will be his nature;*
> *and the nature of all that He creates…*

After his birth He will remember that:

= sophia

> *She is the "Wisdom of Love,"*
> *the wisdom of "Love for ALL life and ALL living,"*
> *For She is Life…who's nature is Love,*
> *the Life and love that fills all that lives.*

> *This great wisdom shall be received by all of creation, a wisdom*
> *that shall be written within the **patterns** of the Soul. It is then*
> *carried by the Mind of Nature, an intrinsically designed*
> *intelligence, woven into the fabric of nature – which becomes the*
> *geometric patterns underlying all forms made manifest.*

Just as we write our ideas on paper, drawing alphabetical tracings of our thoughts…so will the Trinity write his thoughts as the text of nature – geometrical tracings of God's thoughts…

> *These patterns are the thoughts of God from which all things*
> *emerge, **share one mind** – the Mind of Nature.*

> *The Mind of Nature will commune with the mind of the*
> *Trinity Creator, welding with his concepts and ideas…that will*
> *burst forth ignited as Life, made manifest to be loved.*

The Cosmic Mother has now sacrificed all Her creative power and creative aspects to the Trinity. This empowers and further prepares him to go forth in the ***Divine Act of Creation.***

With the Cosmic Mother's enlightened Love and Life understanding, along with Her Breath of Life, She causes a NINTH stage (quality) and step (quantity) toward the engendering of...

The Cosmic Trinity Creator (which will serve as Her spirit)
First Virgin Soul (as Her Soul) and
Creation (as Her body)

And through a chemical and alchemical process (Her love),
*the Eight of Ever-Loving absorbs the VII, VI, V, IV, III, II and then the I, welding them together, and becoming: The Nine Principle of **EVER-BREATHING!***

IX

EVER-BREATHING

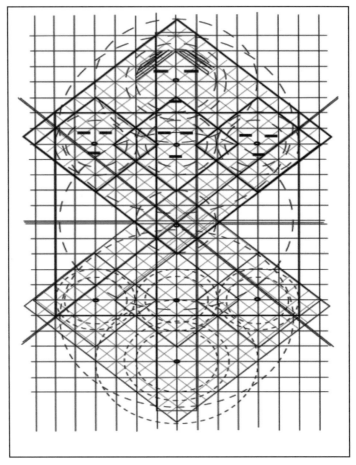

In the **NINTH** step, the ultimate sacrifice is made…

In all Her resplendent glory, the Cosmic Mother looks upon the infants within her womb…

The Arcanum

And as her love bursts forth, She sacrifices herself,
within the flames of Love,
and gives up Her own four-fold, not-self...
Her own Virgin Soul.

The Cosmic Virgin Soul is the core of Her being;
the Breath of Life itself –
Divine LIFE, magnificent, inflamed...
filled by an infinite and selfless desire to share its Love.

Thus, the Causal Mother has allowed Herself
to be completely absorbed by Her own creation...
Her magnetic dark warmth fills, sustains and contains
the infant Trinity Creator, Virgin Soul nature,
and all Creation to come.

We shall remember that...

She is the Immaculate Conception, the first cause, and the origin
of creation – the essence of which has neither beginning nor end.
Unveiled, beyond death, She remains within all that exists,
as the Divine spark from which all will come forth.

This VIRGIN SOUL has no "self" or "spirit-self" in it. It is a purely self-less Love-Aware state of Being...

The Holy Grail:
"Virgin Soul"

205

*And linked to the Virgin Soul, is Her **Soulmind,***
*which is then fused to the **spiritmind** of the Trinity Creator.*

The Soulmind will allow His spiritmind to receive and absorb
the empyreal light of Divine intelligence – whereby the self-
*centered spiritmind can be **redeemed** (or **recreated**), and*
absorbed into the SELFLESS Love essences that go into the
***building of His Soul...** Only through this act of redemption, is*
His Spirit renewed and returned to Her as One.

> *The Soul has a **Soulmind.***
> *The Spirit has a **spiritmind.***
> *The future physical body (within*
> *the creatures of creation)*
> *has a **natural mind**...*

All three must be made purified before returning to the Source.

Purification of the Spiritself

The process of purification of the Spiritself is developed through our attitude and understanding of our Life's experiences. As the Spiritself undergoes and overcomes the hardships of its daily existence, it's spiritmind "charges up," causing emotional (alchemical) and physical (chemical) **heat.**

This heat in turn, burns away the dross materials of our being, clarifying the vision of our natural mind (as understanding), and thus leaving purified Soul essences – essences that are absorbed into the building of our Soul.

The Spiritself will gather these purest of essences, and the chaste of all thoughts, and thereby grow with the understanding gained from the most virtuous acts.

And as the Spirit's self-centered aspects are transformed, the purified Spirit is absorbed by the Soul. The hardened physical body erodes and is made polished, rarified, and refined...and the warmth of the Divine Fire of Life welds these pure essences of the Spiritmind and body into the Soulmind and body – chemically and alchemically; the three (body, mind) and (spirit) are transmuted whereby the Soul is made whole and returns to the One.

It is only through the heat of the Divine Fire of Life that the Spiritself may transform and redeem its self-centered nature. Once purified, the self-centered Spirit can be absorbed into the selfless Virgin State of the Soul.

> ...Of all the world's prefigured destiny,
> Certain this end I know: Love's fire shall purge
> These dreggy crucibles, this dross refine,
> (our bodies and minds – to purify)
> And from corruption draw the gold divine.
> (from mortal dross, we transform then draw pure essences for
> the building of the Soul)
>   – *The Sonnets of GSO #64*

❖

Through a chemical (heat) and alchemical process (Her love)...

The Trinity has now become EVER-BREATHING.
The IX absorbs the VIII, VII, VI, V, IV, III, II and the I...Thus
igniting the TENTH STEP..."X - is - Ten - ce"... "Existence
comes into being!"

X

EXISTENCE

(X-is-Ten) (Ex-is-ten-ce)

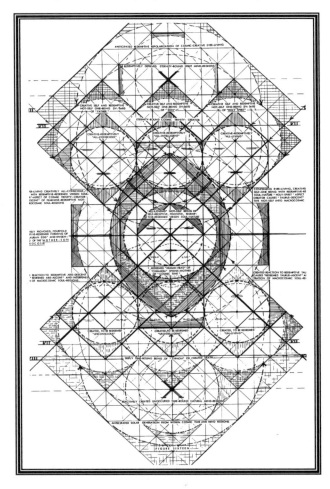

Existence: *The X-shape showing the newly differentiated Cosmic Space: the birth of the Trinity Creator in the Eternity Region (above), the Soul in the Central Soul Region (middle/center) and Primordial Matter in the created Time regions (below).*

The Tenth Dimension comes to manifesting!

With the Tenth Step, the cosmos opened wide...
Her Space-being spreading out in gentle waves
like arms caressing, enveloping the new life
bursting forth from the Empyreal light within Her womb.
In that moment LIFE IS REBORN...
Her generation is carried to birth,
filling all of space (again) with Her being.

The birth of the Cosmic Mother's Spirit, Soul and Body:

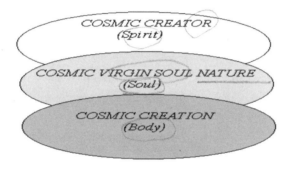

A cry was heard that **echoed** throughout all infinities of space existence... resounding the birth of the **infant TRINITY CREATOR**, born as Her **SPIRIT**, made manifest in the upper Heaven regions of cosmic space.

This is the glory of God...
the birth She had longed for...
Oh how the Cosmic Mother had selflessly desired to give of Her
Love... and now Her dreams are made a true reality...
She is Dreaming True.

This is why we have access to the truths of our Cosmic origins... we share Her memories...She Dreams True, through us.

209

And although the Cosmic Mother is now left creatively exhausted, the Trinity's ever-living "Self-being" shall go on to create all future creators, creatures and creation; for Her memories are infused within their Souls…

*And as the cosmos opened wide, the first infant **VIRGIN SOUL Nature is born.** This is the cosmic Mother's "selfless" aspect…Her SOUL…made manifest in the Central Soul regions of Her inner space! (See diagram.)*

*And as the echo is heard throughout all of space, its cry resounds the light and warmth of the Causal Mother's Life and Love, first dividing itself…its **first contact with form**…heralding the birth of **CREATION…born as Her BODY.***

Creation is made manifest in the lower form regions of cosmic space existence – where we will eventually live and breathe and have our being.

TIME REGIONS
FORMS /CREATION
(*Cosmic space existence* – where we will live)

ETERNITY REGION – HEAVEN
COSMIC TRINITY CREATOR
(*Cosmic Space* – Home environment)

CENTRAL SOUL REGION
COSMIC VIRGIN SOUL
(Inner Space)

Note: the lower, created regions had been left as unconscious, unintelligent and unliving primordial matter – receptive to the birth of Creation, because it hungered for that which was taken away. ✓

Manifesting of the Trinity Creator, Virgin Soul Nature, and Creation in space:

1)	Trinity Creator occupies the upper (four-dimensional rarified) Heaven region of space.
2)	(Area where upper and lower regions overlap) Virgin Soul alone, stays directly connected with the creatively exhausted Cosmic Mother, drawing purely feminine, ever-living and loving, re-creative substances that are used for Virgin Soul growth.
3)	Creation occupies the lower (densified) Form/Time regions of space – filled with Primordial Matter.

❖

The Cosmic infant Trinity Creator has now been carried to birth as a ***triune,*** (self-individualized) Spiritself. Each of the three spiritselves will have a Virgin Soul attached (see illustration.).

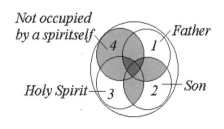

However, because the Cosmic Mother's original Virgin Soul has four aspects, the Trinity only absorbs 3 Souls, thus leaving one Virgin Soul empty, with **no** "self" or **"Spirit + self/ego" in it.** This empty one is left as a selfless, *Virgin Soul Nature* or *Core:*

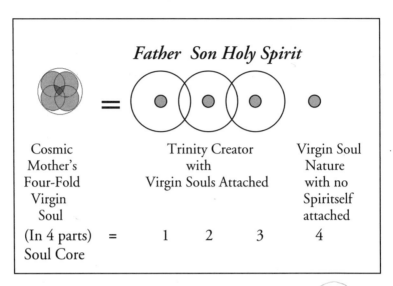

Father Son Holy Spirit

Cosmic Mother's Four-Fold Virgin Soul	Trinity Creator with Virgin Souls Attached	Virgin Soul Nature with no Spiritself attached
(In 4 parts) = Soul Core	1 2 3	4

This Soul Core will later become the fertile **Cosmic Egg** through which all Spirits of creations will become ensouled.

Thus the remaining Soul Nature remains self-less, having no self – Spiritself attached. It will stay open and fertile for continuous Soul bearing and future Spiritself occupancy...the propagating of Souls for ensouling.

The future spirits that will **occupy the Soul** are:
- Self-centered
- Self-serving
- Self-displaying
- Self-expressing
- Self-expending: using up its own life and light

Since the Spiritself is self-expending, it is DEATH creative, subject to eventual death unless it is love or warmth sustained by the warmth of the Cosmic Mother's self-less Virgin Soul. This is why the Spiritself occupies the Soul...to be **sustained** long enough (lifetimes) to be redeemed and recreated into a purified state, whereby it may return to the Source. The process of ensouling, achieving purification, and transformation *is The Divine Plan*...the nature and reason for Involution and Evolution itself.

> *It is through the Soul that we shall stay connected to Her for eternity. She does this, so...*

>> *We may be sustained and contained*
>> *by her Life, and warmth of her Love;*
>> *Experience her being,*
>> *And transform our self-centered Spiritselves*
>> *into the selfless state of the Soul.*

> *Once the Spiritself is perfected, purified, distilled, and finally absorbed by the Soul, the Spirit is restored to its natural state within the Cosmic Mother's being.*

Though the individuated Soul will eventually be reabsorbed by the Oneness, becoming aware of the whole...it retains, through its awareness, a sense of its own relationship to the One – differentiated, but never divided. However, once ALL aspects of God's being have been returned, this ALLness is embraced by the heat of God's love, washing away all sense of differentiation and welded as One...going into a state of rest (to replenish itself)...and then the cycle of recreation begins again.

❖

> *So, with the birth of the Trinity Creator, Virgin Soul, and Creation, the Cosmic Mother is left **creatively exhausted and creates no more!***

Yet a new era is born...and just as we must grow up through infancy, childhood, adolescence, and Soul-maturing, so must the Trinity Creator grow up to His responsibility...of creating the Love and Life dreams of His Cosmic Mother, making them a reality.

Part V

After the
Big Bang

Part V
After the Big Bang
God our Creator
And the Origin of the
Mind of Nature

*All creation is manipulated by **secondary** causes.*
Sir Francis Bacon

This secondary cause is the Trinity using the Mind of Nature.
Marie Bauer Hall

As an artist would mold his clay, the Trinity Creator looks to the mass of ***primordial matter*** to mold His creative ideas into form. Yet as He looks across space existence, all He sees is ***mindless,*** unconscious, unintelligent, and unliving matter – totally unsuitable for the living creations He wishes to set forth.

So the Trinity creates a tool, through which he can work with this *mindless* matter – a vehicle that can penetrate matter to carry back consciousness, intelligence, and living…that vehicle, through which this is accomplished, is the *Mind of Nature*.

Just as the *natural* ***mind*** of man carries his consciousness and intelligence, this **"Mind"** of Nature, carries nature's consciousness, intelligence, and living…permeating matter within all dimensions and form.

The Trinity Creator will link His mind to the Mind of Nature to communicate, project and work with nature…to reform and reshape the primordial matter – *body-mind building ingredients of nature* – into His creations and creatures. Through this process, Life and intelligence is carried back into form, so that it too may evolve and thereby return to the source.

The Mind of Nature

The Mind of Nature itself, is a ***vital etheric*** substance that has two aspects to its nature:

1) It is a (four-dimensional) ***etheric*** (emotional) moisture that can permeate the three dimensions of matter.

2) And it is a (five-dimensional) ***vital vehicle*** that conducts or transmits Life – Life flows through it.

As we shall see in the following pages, the Divine Father, Son, and Holy Spirit will use this Mind of Nature in three different ways:

- The Father, with All-Consciousness emphasis, **conceives** the **Divine Plan of Creation** by remembering the Cosmic Mother's Love and Life dreams.

- The Son, with All-Intelligent emphasis, **expresses the Divine Plan by uttering the Divine Word.**

- The Holy Spirit, with All-Living emphasis, **brings the plan into fruition by infusing** the essence of Life and Light.

The Trinity Creator & the Mind of Nature
First: The All-Conscious Father Conceives the Divine Plan of Creation

The Father, having created the Mind of Nature, conceives the plan of universal creation. Just like building plans for a house, the Father uses the etheric part of the Mind of Nature to draw his plans, or ***etheric image,*** of what form the matter shall take. This etheric image is the underlying ***pattern*** (mathematical and geometric design) within all nature; they are the lines through which life will enter the newly organized form.

For example, if a particular creature were to be created, its *etheric image or pattern* (building plan) would first have to be created by the Father aspect of the Trinity Creator. This (four-dimensional) etheric image or pattern of the future form, then *penetrates matter*, and reawakens the (one-dimensional) energy of life:

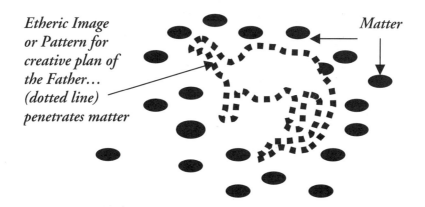

Etheric Image or Pattern for creative plan of the Father... (dotted line) penetrates matter

Matter

Secondly: The Creative All-Intelligent Son
Expresses The Divine Plan By Uttering the Divine Word

Once the Father conceives the Divine Plan of Creation, He transmits his creative plan, sharing it with the Son aspect of the Trinity. The Son becomes so moved, He calls out in the Divine Language, uttering the all-powerful fiat of the *Creative Word*...it *echoes, resonating* through the Mind of Nature, that has already penetrated matter...causing a *resonant trembling* in the etheric mist as *perpetual motion.*

This *echo* or resonant trembling sets one-dimensional energy into motion...thus causing a glowing state of moving energy. This moving energy manifests as (two-dimensional) force in the creation of *physical light.*

And the earth was without form, and void;
and darkness was upon the face of the deep.
And the Spirit of God *moved* upon the face
of the *waters* (etheric sea). And God said,
Let there be light: and there was light.
Genesis I: 2-3

As the *echo* of the creative word continues to resonate through the Mind of Nature, the Form Animating Life Principle (FAL – manifested in Step III) is Divinely moved to follow the etheric image of a form the Father has conceived.

The FAL thereby enters matter, and begins *rearranging its electronic-atomic arrangement* into the molecular arrangements of a 3-dimensional form that matches the etheric plan. Thus causing *molecular differentiation.*

Once the FAL has organized the form, it too becomes an element within the geometric tracing or pattern, running along side the vital etheric Mind of Nature:

The Form Animating Life Principle (FAL) enters matter and starts rearranging it (dark solid line)

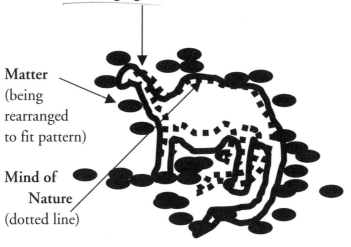

Matter
(being
rearranged
to fit pattern)

Mind of
    Nature
(dotted line)

- *Mind of Nature = Plan/Image*
- *Form Animating Life Principle (FAL)* = *Follows plan, enters matter and rearranges it (causing molecular differentiation) to organize form*

Third: The Creative All-Living Son, the Holy Spirit, Brings the Divine Plan into Fruition

Then the third aspect of the Trinity, the Divine Spirit of the Holy Ghost, contemplates fruition of this plan. He seeks the newly organized form that matches or records the Divine Plan of the Father, and embodies the Divine Sound or Word of the Son.

Upon finding that newly organized form which the Form Animating Life principle has rearranged from within matter, the Holy Spirit then gives of His *all-living*. This vital (five-dimensional) essence of *Life* is so precious and elusive that it quickens the matter as it runs through the etheric four-dimensional aspect of the Mind of Nature.

(Note: A five dimensional aspect, such as Life, cannot directly enter a three-dimensional form. Therefore, the five-dimensional essence of Life uses a four-dimensional [etheric] aspect of the Mind of Nature as a vehicle to enter form.)

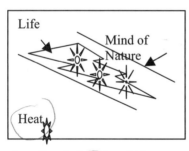

thereby, *deforming Life.*

As Life runs through the etheric Mind of Nature (that has already penetrated matter), it finds that it is an emotional *moisture.* When the heat, carrying the light of Life, contacts this moisture, the *moisture puts the Life light out...*

However, by the time the Life light goes out, the heat (that Life originally brought in with it) has already penetrated the matter and heated it up. This explains why our planet was a swirling fireball and when it cooled off, Life came out of it.

Once the matter is heated, the Form Animating Life Principle takes over…raising the energy/force constitution of form (the make-up of form) to a vibratory rate, which matches the etheric image of what form it will take. And where the Son aspect has organized the matter, the Holy Spirit infuses Life and Divine Intelligence along the lines of that form, and causes the ***molecular division of matter,*** bringing that (three dimensional) form to Life:

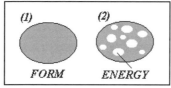

(3) Vital-etheric Mind of Nature (in the image of what that form is to take).

(4) Animating Life Principle "A" enters the form or matter through the four-dimensional Mind of Nature (the Etheric image of what that form should be). The FAL Principle then raises the energy vibration of matter to match the etheric image – causing molecular differentiation.

(5) Then five-dimensional Life runs through the Mind of Nature, running along the lines of this 3 dimensional form, causing molecular division.

FATHER

Expresses Life-Energy I

Conceives Plan:
Drawing a plan or *etheric image* of what form the matter shall take. This is the under-lying *pattern* geometric/mathematical design) within the mind of Nature – the lines through which Life and intelligence will enter the newly organized form.

Creative Wisdom

SON

Expresses Life-Force II

Expresses the Divine Plan by uttering the Divine Word:
Approves, and speaks proposal. Using the Divine Language, He utters the Word of Creation – the word or sound causes internal changes, or molecular differentiation to organize the form.

He issues the Divine Language through the mind of Nature.

Redemptive Wisdom

HOLY SPIRIT

Expresses Life Form III

Brings plan into fruition - infusing the essence of Life:
Contemplates fruition.
He shares his All-Living and intelligence... sending it along the lines of three- dimensional form, and causes the molecular division of matter (so it splits or regenerates i.e. crystal, etc.)

Redemptive Wisdom

The Divine Plan is the blueprint for the
Evolution of Life, intelligence, and form
as it moves toward a purified state –
returning to its Source

Note: Marie had explained that whenever we speak of space and the **three-dimensional** forms of nature, we should include all substances, both visible and invisible, that are consumed in that space. Therefore we must include the cohesive element, which holds the "elemental planetary forms (earth, air, fire, water) in its embrace"...ether. As elemental forms float within this misty sea of universal ether, it is in a constant process of interrelated motion: ever-changing its relationship to space, and its relationship of one form to another...being ever measured by time.

So when we speak of three-dimensional Creation, we can look at it as space, form, and time...held in unison by the mysterious ether. Space is an invisible fourth-dimensional aspect, permeated with this etheric constitution. While time measures the duration of the forming and organizing of matter...beginning with the inception of form and terminating with its perfection.

Please see **Appendix** for Marie's theory on the *Text of Nature. This theory reveals the* process or steps in which a **human author** takes its ideas and writes them down as text; and then compares it to the process through which the Trinity Creator, the **Divine Author**, takes his ideas and manifests them as the forms of nature, which she calls, the ***Divine Text of Nature.***

The Cosmic Trinity Creator and Creation

Each aspect of the multi-dimensional human composite, and all life and living creation itself, has an innate need to evolve. And the evolution of each of these forms (physical, spirit, Soul) is governed by an innate intelligence that lies within the makeup of these forms. This innate intelligence will press *physical form* onward through its own evolution to accommodate and sustain the varying degrees of intelligence (consciousness) that will eventually come to live in these forms. And on an etheric level, (during the earliest stages of form) it will govern the building of the Soulbody as it moves towards the sustaining of a Soul.

But this ensouling and the process of evolution is not only intrinsic to the nature of Creation, but to the Trinity Creator as well, for He too goes through an evolution of being – infancy, childhood, adolescence and Cosmic Soul maturing – to perfect *himself.* And since our Universe is patterned by the nature of *our* Trinity Creator, whom we recognize as the Father, Son, and Holy Spirit, it is logical that, as children of God, the steps and stages that *we* go through in *our* microcosmic human development are reflective of the macrocosmic nature of our patterned Creator.

The Trinity Creator

Within the moment that the Cosmic Mother had brought the Trinity Creator to birth, they were ready to begin Creation. First, the Father conceives the plan of those things He desires to create. Then, the Son utters the Word (sound) that puts that plan into action (organizing matter into the various forms causing molecular differentiation). And then, the Holy Spirit gives life to that form (also causing form division).

Through the creative efforts of the three came multitudes of cosmic form worlds and spirit worlds:

226

When the first, original Trinity Creator began to create, this Trinity created other Trinity Creators, just like himself, who then began to create their own world and family systems. Some collectives were like our own, others different; each ruled by divine Parent/Creators.

Marie discussed this aspect of the cosmology in her book, *The Christ Principle,* where she theorizes the existence of multiple collectives within multiple universes. However, these *other* Trinities and their collectives function independently and are individuated within their own patterns of living.

Our Trinity Creator
Comes to Maturing Within the Cosmic Egg

"Laws and ways of creation (III) are great,
But laws and ways of redemption (IV) are greater."
- Sir Francis Bacon, *Advancement of Learning*

It can be difficult to conceive that our Cosmic Trinity Creator was born as an infant creator, experiencing the early stages of his own natural unfoldment, both consciously and spiritually. Hence, due to this immaturity, the Trinity began creating out of the pressure to create (creative pressure)...and not out of love. To create out of love was a mature act, and being an infant, "all-knowingness" had not yet been fully developed within the Trinity's consciousness.

To develop this understanding of "all-knowingness," the Trinity would have to go through a natural process of growth... experiencing childhood, adolescence and finally, after three eternity-time cycles,[21] He comes to cosmic Soul maturing. With

---

[21] Eternity Time Cycles: 5,000 yr. periods of time; Cycles during the expansion of the Universe.

this Soul maturing, came Self-realization or Enlightenment, which Marie called, their *redemptive repolarization*:

> **Redemptive:** The act of redeeming (purifying) or being recreated through sacrifice and love.
>
> **Re-polarization:** brought back to its original and pure state of One.

In the case of our Trinity Creator, the Son aspect reaches Enlightenment first. And once He has reached Enlightenment, He is instantaneously absorbed into the selfless, Virgin Soul Nature lying within the womb of God.

When the Son aspect, which has a Soul, *joins* with this Virgin Soul Nature, He forms what Marie calls, the ***Mother-Son Macrocosm*** or the ***Cosmic Egg:***

> *Within the Cosmic Egg, the Son aspect experiences all the glories of being at one with the Cosmic Mother. A wholeness and peace fills Him with a love that knows no separation, no emptiness, no division, no beginning and no end. He experiences a feeling of completeness, where the Light of Understanding burns deep within his own Soul...*

> *Through this Enlightenment, the Son sees the Cosmic Mother's former dreams of creation and future beings and creatures that had yet to be born. He sees his own birth and what She had sacrificed for the Trinity to come into being.*

> *But most importantly, the Son aspect realizes that all the Trinity has created thus far was **not** created out of the warmth of Love — but out of the pressure to create. And without the warmth of Love, which is the sustenance of the Soul, these forms (once using up its Life and light) would eventually become deformed Life...its consciousness left to die, and its form (body) left cold, empty, and unpurified, unable to return to its source.*

Once the original four aspects of the Cosmic Mother had welded becoming Life Energy, this newly formed Life ingredient could not return to its original state unless purified within its natural laws of evolution. This natural law of evolution meant ensoulment was necessary because: the Soul is the only aspect to stay directly connected to the Cosmic Mother...the source of all Life and light. Therefore, it is only through ensoulment (with its warmth and Love sustaining aspects of God) that a form or any conscious intelligence that is divided from the source can be sustained long enough to be purified and returned to the Source.

For example, if a Spiritself (Spirit + self/ego) along with its "self"centered consciousness is not sustained by a Soul, it is subject to death. Because the Spiritself moving through lifetimes uses up its own Life and light, there is nothing with which it can replenish itself. Once the Spiritself runs out of Life and light essences, its consciousness or LIGHT goes out...and its LIFE (since it can never die) becomes **deformed Life**, floating about, unable to return to its Source. And if a Life ingredient remains deformed, or separated from its Source, the One can never be made whole again.

The Son aspect has now come to the understanding:

All that had been created, within all categories and Kingdoms will need to be redeemed, purified...and to do this, both Form Worlds and Spirit Worlds will have to journey through the evolutionary Kingdoms of Nature, to be ensouled.

*Once ensouled, both Kingdoms are **infused** with the love-warmth of the Cosmic Mother...whereby Her own Virgin Soul Nature will sustain and contain all of Creation long enough to be redeemed, made purified, and returned to its original virgin state.*

As the Son aspect, who already has a Soul, is joined with the Cosmic Egg of the Virgin Soul Nature, He suddenly comes to the realization that He is in direct alignment with the *source* of all...in other words, He is the result of the very first division of *The One*. Therefore, if He stays within the Soul Core, He will absorb the entire Virgin Soul Nature unto Himself, thus jeopardizing the ensouling of all creation to come.

Without the Virgin Soul Nature, all is lost...for if the Spiritself of the Son absorbs the Virgin Soul Nature for himself, it will loose Its ability to give birth to other Souls.

Without Souls to sustain creation, it would ultimately lead to the deforming of Life.

Because the Son is a three-in-one being, The Father and the Holy Spirit are aware of his experiences – while lying within the Soul Core. And to keep the Son from completely absorbing the Virgin Soul Nature, the Father and Holy Spirit quickly *double up* (unite) their individual Souls, to keep themselves from welding with the Son. The Son aspect is aware of all that has happened...

And with love and understanding of His mission, the Son sacrifices Himself in the second sacrificial Christ Event... giving up his place within the Cosmic Egg.

Relinquishing his Spirit and Soul attainment, the Son sacrifices the warmth of the Soul Nature, and returns to the Father and Holy Spirit.

As a Trinity, the light of understanding experienced through the Son, has flashed throughout the Souls and beings of the Father and Holy Spirit causing their own redemptive-repolarization... Enlightenment!

*And along with the enlightenment of the Father and the Holy Spirit, the Son completes the second sacrificial Christ Event — where all three, understanding their origins, purpose, and destiny, have sacrificed their place within the Soul Core…Now all of creation may return to the Source, **before** them.*

The Trinity is then lead to reinforce the evolution of the kingdoms by sending additional Love-warmth (heat) to ignite the life forms that were ready to make transition into the next kingdom.

*This additional Love-warmth (heat) spreads within all Life and living creatures…within all dimensions, above and below; thus allowing for the most advanced and highest evolved category within each kingdom to **graduate into the next.***

The forms *within* each kingdom, having reached a quality of 100%, were ready to make transition into the next. For the first time, the mineral would make transition to the vegetable kingdom; vegetable seed would move to the Third Kingdom of animal egg; and animal egg would make transition to the womb of Fourth Kingdom, Prehuman Animal Man.

It is important to remember that Spirits, Souls, minds, and bodies were recreated or redeemed as they evolved through the various experiences that each category and kingdom had to offer.

The Trinity, through their sacrifice, had now set evolution into motion — to perfect the things they had originally created, by recreating them out of Love.

*And in that moment, the kingdoms advanced…the Cosmic Cycle ended and the **Solar Cycle began.** The Universe is begun again — this time, recreated out of Love.*

*The Cosmic Trinity Creator, who had grown up through infancy, childhood, adolescence, and Cosmic Soul maturing, would now be called the **Solar Redeemer Creator** – working toward the redeeming of all life and living intelligence.*

With the onset of the Solar Cycle, Cosmic Spirit Worlds and Form Worlds were redeemed and recreated. And all Life involutionary and form evolutionary categories and Kingdoms, advanced – coming to solar planetary RECREATION, whereby all Life was recapitulated and recreated…initiating the start of a new Solar Planetary scale.

I wonder if this is why the cataclysmic occurrence and the so-called extinction of the dinosaurs during the Paleolithic age had taken place. Were their physical forms not conducive to the new solar era that was born?

Part VI

The
Evolution of Kingdoms

EVOLUTION OF KINGDOMS

The Two Collectives Come to Ensouling...

The Spirit Worlds
and
Form Worlds Below

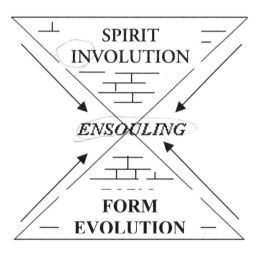

*The two inverted pyramids symbolize the two prehuman categories that came to ensouling: 1) The **spirits descending** – Angelic beings descending from the heavens to be embodied and ensouled, and... 2) the **forms ascending** – mineral, plant, animal, Prehuman animal-man ascending to be ensouled. Both groups are unequal in their beginning forms, and will only be born equal when they come to ensouling.*

I found Marie's explanation of the evolution of man to be one of the most exciting aspects of this work. Up to now, I knew there were the Evolutionists of science and the Creationists of religion, that for centuries, have argued the question as to how man had first come to walk the earth. Did he evolve through the evolution of the kingdoms to his present state, i.e. *Mineral – Plant/Vegetable – Animal – Human?* Or are we, the result of a long line of descendants of the Biblical Adam and Eve whose spirits descended from the heavens to walk within the Garden of Eden?

In this work, both creation and evolution became valid arguments, both working on different dimensions **at the same time.** The concept of Adam and Eve related to the **spirits** *descending* **to become ensouled,** and the ancient hominid, related to the **forms** *ascending* **to be ensouled.**

Forms Ascending

The first, category represents the **forms** *ascending.* These forms ascend from the ground or mineral kingdom up the evolutionary ladder to be ensouled:

Kingdoms of Nature
6ᵗʰ Kingdom – Immortal Man
5ᵗʰ Kingdom – Human (Ensouling)
4ᵗʰ Kingdom (Prehuman) Animal-Man
3ʳᵈ Kingdom – Animal
2ⁿᵈ Kingdom – Plant/Vegetable
1ˢᵗ Kingdom – Mineral

The ancient hominid, whose families walked the Earth millions of years ago, was part of these forms *ascending.* And because they were perfecting the physical body, mind, and senses, as they moved *up* the evolutionary ladder, they are called the *Natural-selves.*

Cro-Magnon man was a natural-selfhood – in a pre-*human* state of living called ***Animal-man*** (4th Kingdom). Animal-Man, though advanced enough in evolution to have developed the first stages of their Soulbodies and Soulminds, had not yet been *quickened* or fully ensouled.

In the early stages of Animal-man, his Soulbody and Soulmind, and Spirit were still being prepared for the Soul to be attached, while the physical brain and other organs were being developed to sustain higher states of consciousness. Only a fully developed, Prehuman Animal-man could make transition to the next kingdom, where Spirit, Soul and minds are *quickened* within the human form.

Pre-human, Animal-man was the missing link, making a giant leap both intellectually and physically after his ensouling. And became what was known as a Fifth Kingdom "Human" state of living.

Once ensouled, the form-ascended Prehuman Animal-man of the Earth incarnate as the gentle Souls, generally passive and very much connected to the earth.

Spirits Descending

The second category of human evolution represents the **spirits descending.** They are the **Prehuman Spiritselves** descending from the heavens to be ensouled.

The Prehuman Spiritselves include the spirits of the Biblical Adam and Eve, Archangels, and the personalities of the archetypal Gods and Goddesses of mythology. This group, the Spirits descending, were *forming* and *developing* their spirit and Soul bodies and minds as they went through the evolution of the Spirit Kingdoms. And although their *consciousness* was being developed – and some to a most advanced degree – they too were not yet ensouled! Complete ensouling did not begin until the first "Man and Woman," the biblical/archetypal *Adam and Eve.* Hence, Adam and Eve became the *progenitors* of the collective on Earth, through which both Prehuman Spiritselves and Natural-selves would come to ensouling.

Once ensouled, these Prehuman Spiritselves generally incarnate as very strong and determined or sometimes ego-centered individuals, seemingly driven. This may be a *hangover* from their Prehuman development in that the Prehuman Spiritselves (without the limitations of the physical body) have had more time to develop consciously within their spirit-body and spirit-mind *building* than the Natural-selves who ascend from the Earth. The Natural-selves, having spent more time *within* the natural development of their physical forms, are generally more developed physically and more receptive to the natural worlds. However once the Natural and Spiritselves are ensouled, they are born equally into the human experience. This has no bearing on cultural development. There are Spirtselves and Natural-selves in all cultures.

Selfhoods of Both Collectives

Within the earliest stages of creation before Adam and Eve, Prehuman Spiritselves and Natural-selves were still only Fourth Kingdom selfhoods, not yet quickened by a Soul. And although, both Form ascending and Spirit descending Prehuman groups are creatively endowed with a creative consciousness, both selfhoods (Spiritselves and Natural-selves) will move through their evolutionary kingdoms, with different challenges to overcome.

The Forms Ascending Within the Natural Worlds

Spirit Involution
Spirits Descending to Ensoulment

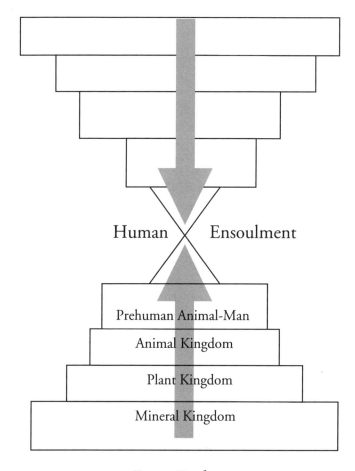

Form Evolution
Forms Ascending Through the Kingdoms to be Ensouled

The Perfection and Transition
Within the Kingdoms of Nature

"Seize me, seize me ere I die; I am the Life"
Testament of Beauty

God is Life…infused within all of nature.
Moving…alive…Glorious Life…expressing Itself in motion
while experimenting with the forms within the Kingdoms of
Nature.

And the further Life moves along the evolutionary ladder, the
more complex the forms, for they are innately driven…moving
towards their own perfection…modeling the perfection of the
*very **Life within!***

Life imprisoned within form, expresses Itself in the measured
motion of evolution. And as Life evolves, it is ever-seeking its
freedom from form…seeking the path that returns to its source.

The more perfect the forms, the higher they are within the
kingdoms, for each kingdom is clearly defined from one another
by their qualities and abilities. As an example:

When Life sought out the qualities of keen eyesight through
which the eyes would be perfected…the Eagle emerged. As Life
sought out the qualities of acute hearing…the Dolphin emerged.

As a form moves through the kingdoms, there is a formula,
a definite measure, of *Life Energy* (force and other substances) that
are absorbed by the forms within each category differentiating
their constitution from one another. And when the measured
amount of Life Energy runs out in a form, *death* occurs.

240

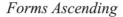

In rebirth, the new form not only takes on a higher state of development, it innately carries with it the more refined qualities and characteristics, good or bad, acquired in its previous form. Here is where *Karma* comes into play.

Each form within the kingdoms evolved from a quality of 1-100%. Upon reaching 100%, or state of perfection, a form then made transition into the next kingdom in its evolutionary path. And as we will see, within each additional kingdom, Life took on a vehicle that became more efficient and complex:

> *The kingdoms evolved during cycles of planetary days and nights. And the forms, inspired by Life, slowly made their way up through the form worlds, its innate intelligence choosing amongst the different categories within each kingdom... searching for a form that would provide it with the various experiences through which each of its senses and organs could be further developed.*

The First: Mineral Kingdom

The process of evolution began. The magnificence of Life, the hand of God, moved like fingers in motion, molding the substance we call primordial matter...purifying it chemically and alchemically, using energy, force, and the most purified of form and etheric substances.

Then Life began creating paths to organize these forms; and these paths took on patterns through which Life and intelligence danced...thrilled and eager to share Its Love.

*With Love **inflamed**, the earthy mineral substance of form hungering for this love absorbed the heat, making it more pliable, reorganizing its constitution...bringing it to a more refined state.*

*In time, the substances of the mineral kingdom began to evolve through its own **experiences and heat.***

And just as man goes through life's experiences of pain, anguish, joy and peace to perfect oneself – our mineral goes through the heat, cold, and pressures of the Earth.

As man is slashed by the pounding of life upon his spirit and Soul, so does the rain and thunder pound and slash at that mineral that lies within the Earth, perfecting it...moving it from a 1st degree of organization...onward to higher degrees within the mineral kingdom – that of silver, gold, and diamond.

Then finally, upon reaching the highest degree of its perfection – at a 100% – the mineral becomes the Crystal.

The crystal's agitation or heat can be compared to human suffering. However, since heat cannot be separate from light, this suffering or heat, is ALWAYS compensated with the same degree of light. In man, this light comes as understanding:

> *As the crystal's agitation builds, the heat of the supernal light is absorbed into the crystal form, making it purified, lighter, and more transparent.*

> *This is the same as in the suffering of man, for he too, is compensated with the same degree of light: The more he suffers, the heat of Love chemically and alchemically transforms his being, abating the dross materials, firing out his imperfections.*

> *And the more heat brought on by his suffering, the more he is compensated with the lighting of his intelligence...as Divine Understanding.*

Note: The crystal is one of the few minerals in its kingdom to contain an element in man called silica – and the only one in the kingdom that multiplies or generates itself by division.

> *The fire, air, water, and earth have penetrated the crystal, which has now become a perfectly organized mass. This produces heat within the interior of the crystal form setting the tiny particles within the crystal into motion...bringing it to an even higher degree of organization.*

> *With each step that nature takes, there is a building of a body and mind...The interior body of the crystal goes through a metamorphosis, whereby the origin and evolution of man's reason and emotion begin.*

> *The rational is seen in the geometric shapes of the crystal – which is influenced by the **light** belaboring it; while emotions are*

*revealed in the colors of the crystal – affected by the **warmth** belaboring it.*

Within the Principle of Life, lies the inherent state of perfection...

And as the mineral evolves as a crystal, each of the smaller baby crystals (in the image of the mother crystal) has slowly become independent of the mother crystal, until they too, are perfected and ready to be set free.

When the crystal form has reached its goal, at the highest degree of perfection (100%), **it has resolved and consumed its own limitations,** and is ready to make transition into the next kingdom:

The crystal now experiences a timeless suspension, where through the Mind of Nature, it becomes aware of its own inner perfection and eternal destiny.

Upon seeing its destiny and a vision of its own potential of perfection, the form is energized. It reviews its past experiences and welds them, chemically and alchemically, into its nature. Thus, the transformation begins!

*With the crystal in its perfected state, the **Holy Spirit**, the Giver of Life, comes down and gives of His All-Living...running along the lines (or avenues) of the crystal...sharing Life with its perfect tiny crystal forms. Now, the form is impelled to absorb the next quality and degree of Life Energy, whereby it is given the capacity to make transition into the next kingdom.*

At that moment, the tiny crystals are quickened, split away from the mother crystal...and these newly independent, baby crystals, lying within the earth, become the receptacles for the seed from which the plant shall evolve and come forth.

The chemical and alchemical elements of the crystal are the basic ingredients necessary for its evolution into the plant Kingdom.

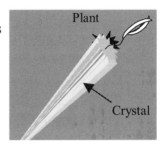

Life produces form, and molds it by its very motion...

Note: 1) The plate from Charles Bonnet ('Oeuvres d'histoire naturelle et de philosophie', 1781) shows the crystal formation at the very lowest step on the ladder of being. 2) It has been said that vapors coming from the earth, and running down the lines along the forms of the crystal, create a new substance which exists, in human life. Could the Holy Spirit be a metaphor for this vapor?

Life Evolves from the Mineral to the Second:
Plant & Vegetable Kingdom

*As Life moves toward ensouling within the **second** Kingdom of Plant and Vegetables, the perfected little seeds have sprung free of their old form and limitations of the crystal formation. As a plant, though limited in intelligence, it knows how to draw its own nourishment that lies within the unregenerate earth. And because it is limited to stationary growth, the seed is forced to respond to the environment around it.*

The warmth of the earth becomes the womb for the seed, and the seed begins to sprout...it shoots a palette stalk through the earth, and sculptures its way in search of the warmth and light of the sun and air.

Upon piercing the earth's crust, it takes the yellow and gold of the sun and blue of the air, and combines these energies to make the green of the Earth.

The forces of heat and light upon the plant *create a primitive sense-reaction* that influences the coloring and shape that the plant will take. These influences of color, shape, and limited motion, will determine the plant's experiences within form...supporting its progress from the lowest (1%) to the highest degree (100%) of organization within the plant kingdom.

The Fruit

As the plant moves toward a state of 100% perfection it becomes the *moist fruit*. The organization within the fruit is so perfect, that it can not only draw the essence of Life within itself, but the seed of the fruit has the ability of propagation by division...self-reproduction.

When the fruit seed is ripe, the fruit falls from the tree onto the earth below. There it begins to sprout its own stalks that penetrate the earth to form its own roots — the child has walked away from the mother plant. It has begun self-motion and took off to create a new life on its own.

And once the fruit form has reached its goal, at the highest degree of perfection (100%), it has again resolved and consumed its own limitations, and is ready to make transition into the next kingdom. With its spiritbody and Soulbody further developed...

The evolution within the plant and vegetable kingdoms is now complete. Life's shackles within the plant kingdom are dissolved, and its two-dimensional motion of growth and its reaction to its environment, as color, will begin its true development within its next stage.

Our fruit now experiences a timeless and suspended state of vegetable nirvana, where through the Mind of Nature, it sees its destiny and a vision of its own potential moving toward the perfection of its Source.

With this, the form is energized, reviewing its past experiences welding them, chemically and alchemically, into its nature. And the transformation begins again.

*The form is impelled to absorb the next quality and degree of Life Energy, whereby it is given the capacity to make transition into the next kingdom. With Life welded into the newly charged form of the animal kingdom, the fruit with its warmth and moistness will provide the womb that will carry the vegetable seed to its next stage of Life...that of the **animal egg**.*

Life Evolves from the Plant to the Third:
Animal Kingdom
Making Transition from Egg to Womb

*As Life moves toward ensouling within the **third** or Animal Kingdom, It experiments with the beauty, strength, and innocence that lay within the different animal forms.*

As an animal form, Life is set free to respond to its new environment acquired with the experience of *three*-dimensional self-movement (or self-mobility). And although there is no self-individualization as yet, we begin to see the development of the mind and the organs of the **senses.** It is through the coordination of the animal-mind and its senses, and how they relate to the animal form in motion, that we begin to see the building of the primitive animal brain.

The development of the brain and organs of the *senses* plays a key role within the animal kingdom. It is the animal's most important and most strenuous task. The basic sensory organs developed within the previous plant kingdom have to be brought to the next stage. But, unless there is a division of the forms, as male and female, this cannot be done – because certain organs can only be strengthened within one or the other sex...so both must be refined.

The division of the sexes begins with the division of form into male and female, *plus and minus, active and passive body creating electrical tension between their forms.* This *tension* heightens the senses, thereby building and strengthening the organs. The animal's first reaction to this tension is through *color* (including monotones or shades of grays). Thus color and contrast become the next attraction between the male and female species.

248

Forms Ascending

When the divided forms respond to color by reuniting in procreation, it further sharpens the organs of the senses, and specific organs begin to perceive *pain from pleasure.* Once the animal perceives this, the message is sent to a *sensory reflection* at a centralized point where it is coordinated within the brain.

Primitive emotion, "sensual intelligence," then distinguishes between pain and pleasure by responding to it with *sound.* Now, with this new sense reaction (sound), plus the newly developed sense organs (that know pain from pleasure), the animal is not only allowed to associate pain and pleasure with colors, sounds and smells, but with *textures* as well. These new sense *experiences* of the animal are a form of *primitive observation.*

This primitive observation causes the animal to react both emotionally and rationally, and each time there is a reaction, the animal-mind further bonds with its senses and we begin to see the organization of a rudimentary brain. It is the brain organ that allows an animal to communicate with the *Mind of Nature* as **instinct.**

In the lower developed species, Animals merely reflect what is around them. They are not yet creatively endowed. However, within the higher developed species, the brain is more finely organized and ideas begin to play on it from the outside. The developed brain of the animal becomes susceptible to suggestion and gradually develops a degree of intelligence *without* imitation.

As the animal's sense perception develops, the brain becomes the *seat of intelligence* and the animal's physical form develops tendencies toward an upright alignment. And just as the animal spirit is further developed physically, as it moves toward ensoulment, there is also further development of its Soulbody and mind.

The animal form, now perfected reaching 100%, merges with the motivating Life Principle within it, where it is consumed and recharged with a new quality of Life Energy.

Here, for just a moment, the animal experiences its perfection within, an animal Nirvana where time ceases to exist and its desire to meet its destiny is re-ignited.

*The animal's Soul, Spirit, and physical **bodies** receive the Breath of Life…whereby the animal is given creative endowment – the **creative consciousness used by** the self – thus, the animal makes transition to fourth kingdom **Pre-human, ANIMAL-man**.*

(The transition from the Third to Fourth Kingdom within creation takes place during the formation of the Mother-Son Macrocosm or Cosmic Egg.)

The Fourth Kingdom Natural Selfhoods: Prehuman Animal-Man, The Ancient Hominid

Within the Fourth Kingdom, Prehuman Animal-Man will struggle to obtain rulership over his own *animal nature* and environmental nature at large. The animal in him learns to become human, and the man in him learns to conquer his own animal nature. This means everything he had learned in the Animal Kingdom would be relearned, as Prehuman Animal-Man – for the lesser state must be conquered to reach a higher one.

His features are unrefined, sometimes appearing brutish and savage…like the coarseness of the earth from which his body had come.
He is strong and wild like the beast…
still governed by primeval appetites, waiting to be tamed.

At first, his world is quiet like a temple; his mind drifts; his eyes
open wide to nature.
And with wonder and joy, he begins to self-consciously
experiment with his free will...that bring on experiences designed
to further develop his reason and emotions.

The development and perfection of reason and emotion are
Animal-man's primary concerns. By achieving balance he
prepares the way for his ensouling and creative regeneration (the
building of his creative consciousness) and the perfecting of his
Spirit.

As Life's experiences flood his being, emotions are stirred within
him, and he begins to learn. Life becomes his school, and with
the onset of knowledge, additional forms of expression are needed
— whereby his reason begins to take shape and form.

The animal sounds become concepts, then ideas. Ideas turn into
themes, and man begins to use his imagination...developing
beliefs through which his religions will come.

Then suddenly the hardships of life become like flames that lick
upon his sore body...and man's innocence turns to animal
instinct to survive — furthering the development of his self-
consciousness and challenging his Spirit.

His hands and lips crack from the sun; the rain slashes upon his
brow. His innocence is washed away by the seas of darkness
carried by his mind, for he does not understand...why the pain?
Life grows bleak and bare...all emotions are released...beyond
weeping, he can endure no more.

Forms Ascending

As Prehuman animal-man moves through the process of evolution, the *coarseness* of his nature is soothed through the interaction of *Life, motion* and *form*. These experiences cause the constitution of his being to be heated from 1 to 100%, whereby his Soul and etheric *vehicles* are made complete – brought to its highest degree.

His suffering, nature's only crime, becomes a beacon drawing the heat from which he is made purified...and his natural mind, body, spirit, and Soul is set free...For Life sees all he has come to bear, and like the warmth of the sun, sends Love to soothe him – while the light of God's intelligence, nurtures his mind – transforming his very being.

...Until Love's sun fires out our imperfection,
and draws this sphery Soul from shapeless clay.
Sonnets of GSO

And once his faculties of consciousness and organs (being developed through life's experiences) reach 100%, his Soulbody and Soulmind are prepared for complete ensouling.

Prehuman Animal Man is given an additional degree of light (heat), until at its glowing point, he achieves a temporary state of perfection ...where he stands witness to his destiny.

His body and mind is energized. He reviews his past experiences, welding them chemically and alchemically into his nature...and at that point, a second heat[22] is struck...
The lesser form is sacrificed at the expense of a higher degree of Life, for the miracle of Life seeds in death...
Birth, death, and rebirth.

---

[22] Second heat: the lesser form is sacrificed to move to a higher degree of life. (See glossary.)

And a chemical union welds his emotions and reason with the active and passive forces of his being, allowing him to absorb the next quality and degree of Life Energy...

Thus Animal-man is given the capacity to make transition into the next kingdom...causing a new quality of life. His Spiritself becomes attached to his Soulbody and Soulmind. Hence Animal-man becomes Human...quickened and fully ensouled.

> This mind perisheth with this body,
> unless the personal coordination of its ideas
> have won to Being higher than animal life
> at that point, where the ring cometh upward to
> reach the original creative energy, which is God,
> with conscience entering into life everlasting.
>
> *Testament of Beauty*

> These are **THE GENERATIONS OF THE HEAVENS AND OF THE EARTH** when they were created, in the day that the Lord God made the Earth and the Heavens, And every plant of the field before it was in the earth, and every herb of the field before it grew...   Genesis 2:4

The Fifth Kingdom Human

Man is a complex, multi-dimensional composite of mind, body, Spirit and Soul. And each of these aspects is evolving through the Kingdoms of Nature, within both spirit *and* form worlds, at the same time.

Each aspect of man's being is contained within its own vehicle or form: The physical body is a form, the Spirit has a spirit-body for its form, and the Soul has a vital/life essence or Soulbody for its form:

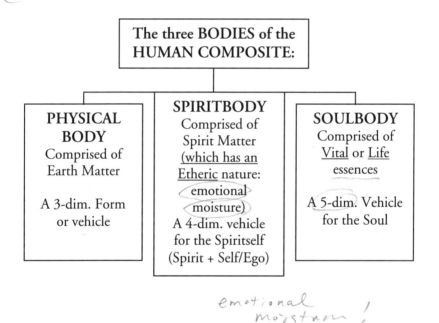

The three BODIES of the HUMAN COMPOSITE:

PHYSICAL BODY
Comprised of Earth Matter

A 3-dim. Form or vehicle

SPIRITBODY
Comprised of Spirit Matter (which has an Etheric nature: emotional moisture)
A 4-dim. vehicle for the Spiritself (Spirit + Self/Ego)

SOULBODY
Comprised of Vital or Life essences

A 5-dim. Vehicle for the Soul

The human composite is also comprised of a multi-dimensional, three-fold mind:

- The physical body has a **natural mind**
- The Spirit has a **spiritmind**; and
- The Soul has a **Soulmind**

And each has its own faculties to be developed:

THE HUMAN COMPOSITE
and its Three-fold Mind

NATURAL MIND
Physical nature – 3-dimensional

- Occupies the physical body.
- Uses trial and error thinking.
- Absorbs the general memories of everyday existence alongside fleeting thoughts.
- These general memories are bound to the physical form (locked in the natural mind) so at death, the physical body and NATURAL MIND, along with its memories return to the body and mind of the Earth – either as a regenerating or degenerating factor depending on the quality of life.

▼

SPIRITMIND
Etheric nature – 4-dimensional

- Occupies the spiritbody of the Spiritself (Spirit + Self) that is attached to a Soul.
- Spiritmind uses **CONSCIOUSNESS** as the light factor of its intelligence (i.e. light bulb (mind), electricity (consciousness).
- Absorbs the memories that are life changing or influential towards the evolution, imprint and purification of the individual.
- These memories are bound to the spiritmind & body, and are taken with us from lifetime to lifetime.

▼

SOULMIND
Vital/Life nature – 5-dimensional

- Occupies the Soulbody, of the Soul, which is the only one that stays connected to the Source.
- Soulmind uses AWARENESS as the life and light sustaining factor of its intelligence.
- Absorbs only the purest of essences…memories that serve as a Divine **blueprint**, influencing all further development and incarnations of any being or form…record keeper.

Physical Body & Mind

Each aspect of man's composite nature is comprised of its own PATTERNS OF LIFE AND LIGHT. These lines of Life and light are the pathways through which Divine intelligence communicates and influences nature. When the Spirit pattern (through goodness and purity) aligns itself to the Soul's divine pattern it perfects the physical form. And when the perfected physical form, upon its death, returns to the Earth, this original vital-etheric pattern remains with the Spirit and Soul…influencing the physical bodies of future incarnations.

Though the design of this vital-etheric pattern changes, as it moves toward a state of perfection, the **central pattern** or blueprint (carried within the Soulbody/mind) always remains the same. This is called "GOD POINT", the immutable design at the central point within the pattern of any created form – within any dimension.

When the Spirit approaches a new incarnation, this newly developed vital-etheric pattern will then reorganize physical matter, causing it to realign itself to this new vital-etheric form – hence, generally speaking, a higher developed physical body for the being (or one suited for further Soul growth. (See: Freewill, fate, and destiny – Arcanum Step VII.)

Spiritbody & Mind

The Spiritself (Spirit + Self/Ego) has a spiritbody and spiritmind. It uses *consciousness* for its intelligence, which is limited and subject to death unless sustained by the love-warmth and awareness of the Soul. The consciousness of the Spiritself is limited, because it is Life and light expending, using up its own Life and light ingredients, going into an unconsciousness state to replenish itself.

The Spiritself is "self" centered and will take lifetimes of creatively conscious mind and body-building (regeneration) to be transformed and absorbed into the "selfless" essences of the Soul.

Because the spirit pattern naturally aligns itself, and is absorbed into, the pattern of the Soul, both Spirit & Soul bodies and minds stay with us at death. Hence, whenever the Spirit's and Soul's body and mind patterns have completely affixed itself to one another, in perfect order, it is quickened by the Soul; thus we experience a sense of nirvana…existence beyond limitation.

Soulbody & Mind

The Soulbody and mind is the immortal, vital or Life forms of the "selfless" Soul. The Soul is the *matrix* of our being, a five-dimensional *patterned* body of Life and light. It is the seat of *awareness*, which is the light and Life *sustaining* factor of intelligence; and is the only aspect of our being that stays directly connected to the Source.

The Soul stays with the unpurified (self-centered) Spiritself, sustaining its consciousness long enough to become purified and absorbed into the selfless state of the Soul. Remember, if the Spiritself is left impure, it becomes deformed life…unable to be reabsorbed by the One.

❖

Though the theories of quantum physics have provided us with cell phones, portable computers and more, its theories have generally been used for technological advances within our Fifth Kingdom living. But what sort of impact do these same theories have on our spiritual or metaphysical planes of existence? What are its phenomenal implications, which have caused some scientists to cringe?

David Deutsch, a world leading theoretical physicist, didn't know he'd be opening a can a worms when he deduced that although quantum theory may appear outlandish, if particles of electrons can exist in many places at once, why can't *mass*, made up from these very particles, do the same? "The theory's laws must hold at every level of reality,"[23] says Deutsch. This meant that not only are we multi-dimensional beings, but we ourselves "have twin counterparts in a nearly infinite number of other universes"…there's a *you* reading this book; there's a *you* that is resting; a *you* that is painting; a *you* that decided to go out with friends and…ad infinitum – countless possibilities.

Now consider this…as Fifth Kingdom Human, living in a vast and rich "multiverse," each of our "selves" (incarnations) are moving toward completion – conscious immortality, a process that enables the being to **sustain** itself within a purely selfless state of **awareness**. The question is, which one of our "selves" will awaken first? And…which life, will that Aware "self" choose to exist within? (See: *New Dimensional Thinking*, Jennings.)

Here are a few suggestions for the Spiritself to sustain the awareness of the Soul: a) Discipline – (i.e. exercise, food, work) draws the heat to purify, conditions the mind and body. b) Distinguishing between the spiritself and Soul – helps us to recognize the various realities within which we live and move. The act of *observing* the self moves us out of a "self-"centered state, into a "Soul-"centered state of awareness through which we can view or observe the self. Only by leaving the self, can we view it. This shows us that we can function within a different perspective or view, using our Soulminds…thus revealing the essence of an unlimited, intelligent "awareness" that lies within this pure state of *Being*. Once achieved, this immortalized being will move into a Sixth Kingdom state of living…a state which has no need for the physical body; and is aware of its existence within many planes. The immortalized "self," no longer self-centered, but Soul or love-centered now becomes the blueprint for the lower selves to follow and emerge within. Remember however, the immortalized being resides within a timeless state. (Detailed later.)

---

[23] Hugh Everett originator of multiverse concept, 1957. See article: Discover Magazine September 2001, by Tim Folger: Quantum Shmantum…David Deutsch.

As we have seen, the natural forms of the lower *(created)* regions were purified and redeemed by ascending through the kingdoms of the form world to be ensouled. However, simultaneously within the upper *(creative)* Spirit regions, there was a birth of spirit worlds and a third stage of transition within the organization of the Spirit regions of our solar system. And as we will see, these fourth-dimensional spirit forms that occupied the upper regions were purified and redeemed by moving through a different evolutionary path to ensouling.

The Spirits Descending Within the Spirit Regions

Spirit Involution
Spirits Descending to Ensoulment

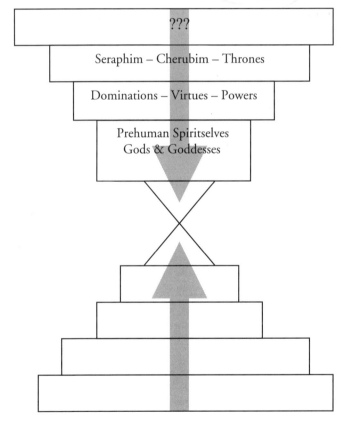

Form Evolution
Forms Ascending Through the Kingdoms to be Ensouled

The Son aspect of the Trinity Creator had uttered the Divine Word…activating the Form Animating Life Principle III. (See Step III of Arcanum.)

The Form Animating Life Principle then began to shape, reform, and reorganize primary organic vehicles out of the elements of nature…thus; creating electric elemental spirit forms…beings predominantly of air (Sylphs), and fire (Salamanders).

The Spiritminds of these *Elemental forms* (spirits of the elements) were fundamental to the development of the animal forms within the natural kingdoms. These advanced Elementals, or group spirits, were sent to regulate the bodily incarnations of the animals in the lower created regions…

The Elementals were the servants of God (mind creatures), studying each form with its various attributes, and then deciding in which bodily form the animal's transition would best be served…

The Elemental Spirits, in perfecting the animal form, were responsible for developing "dual mind-bodies:" A *physical* body for the brain-backed natural mind, and a spirit body for the spiritmind.

The Elemental Mind Creatures would orchestrate the animal's evolution, belaboring and fashioning the forms from without. But while working so closely with the belaboring of the animal's forms something remarkable happened:

*The Elemental Mind Creatures began to draw **subtle form essences** from the animal forms themselves. These subtle form essences became the Elemental's very own etheric counterparts.*

Spirits Descending

Etheric counterparts were the Elemental's *own four-dimensional* vehicle (pattern for the natural world) onto which their spirit and future Soul would be attached. And when the etheric bodies of both, the Elementals and the natural kingdoms, were advanced enough to make transition into the next:

> *The Holy Spirit projected Life (a five-dimensional aspect) and His All-Living (six-dimensional) into the created region below. Here it entered into the Elemental's etheric (four-dimensional) counterparts (created forms), bringing with it added intelligence. And with the addition of these Life ingredients and heat, the lower created region became a whirling solar nucleus...*

> *Within the **upper** etheric region, Universal Mind, with its intelligence, was welded with the Life...and the creation of the first **pre-human** spirit life-wave (group or collective) of Spiritselves were born – in both spirit and natural form worlds.*

The Elemental Mind Creatures, through the building and purifying of their *own* etheric bodies, *were now* highly attenuated, or advanced enough to enter these newly built Spirit forms...

> *Some of these entities would become a **spirit counterpart**, a Prehuman Spiritself (i.e. mineral spirit, plant, or animal spirit) **without** a physical form.*

> *Others chose to enter into the evolutionary process as spirits **with forms**, attaching themselves to the natural forms of the Earth as: mineral spirits, plant, and animal spirits, or the spirits of the newly built Pre-human Animal-man.*

> *Still others chose to attach themselves to planetary bodies, becoming the Spirits that occupied the planets and stars...*

These spirits that occupied planetary bodies were able to evolve through the creatures that inhabited or became ensouled upon their sphere. For example, the *physical* form of the Earth (Earth matter) is what *our* physical body and mind is primarily built from. And upon our death, our bodies and minds are relinquished to return to the Earth from which it had come. At this point, depending on whether we have evolved or not, our essences will either supplement to the building or regressing of the body and mind of the Earth, and its Spirit. Thus, with our help, the physical body of the Earth Spirit is redeemed and purified, allowing for its *own* evolution and regeneration.

Prehuman Spiritselves
And
The Origins of Man

When Marie began speaking about the Angelic life-waves I was quite surprised to find aspects of **mythology** delicately woven throughout her story of *The Bible*. She had applied and aligned the relationships within the dominant Greco-Roman mythologies with early Christianity into a delicate creation myth that would reveal the origins of the archetypes (patterns) of man. Also included were important keys to their relationships, which Marie discovered in the *Cabala.*

What you are about to read is not a human experience; this creation myth began within a Spirit realm in which three-dimensional form, as we know it, did not exist.

In Marie's estimation these newly developed life-waves, were to become **Pre-human Spiritselves (Spirit + self/ego)** – entering these newly built **Pre-human Spiritbodies** as the Archangels, and archetypal Gods or Goddesses. Some of these Spiritselves had previously been the very Elementals and mind creatures that orchestrated the bodily incarnations of the animal kingdom. This would explain their predisposition towards dominance over the natural form worlds – leading to their development of arrogance and self-centeredness often depicted in myths and fables.

Marie had referred to these various Spiritselves, including the Mind spirits, Air spirits, and what was known as the mythological Birdmen, as the *Elderson Collective*. They went through their *(pre-human)* development upon the planet whose concrete remains are now the planet **Venus,** as well as its unregenerate portion, which became our Moon.

265

When I had asked her what these Spiritselves were like, she explained, that these Angels, Gods, and Goddesses, though Prehuman Spiritselves, were actually quite human-like in appearance, making it easy for Eve (Garden of Eden) to be beguiled. They were lucid and bright, very much in the image of their creator. And just like their counterparts (Prehuman Animal-man) these Spiritselves had consciousness, but were not yet ensouled. Their Soulbodies and minds were being developed, but actual ensouling (the attaching of a Spiritself to a Soul), did not begin until the Cancer Eternity Time Cycle and the origin of the "First Man and Woman," the Biblical/archetypal Adam and Eve.

As mentioned before, a Spiritself without a Soul has no way of sustaining itself long enough to be purified. And because the Spiritself is self-expending (using up its own life and light), once it runs out, it is subject to death – its consciousness or light goes out; and its Life (which can never die) if left impure, becomes deformed Life – floating about, unable to return to its Source. If Life ingredients remain deformed, or separated from its source, the One can never be made whole again.

The Creation Myth

Her story begins in the Cancer astrological sub-cycle of the Fourth Great Eternity Time Cycle – long after the birth of the Trinity Creator – long before man comes into existence...

There were three brothers known as:
*The **Father aspect of the Trinity Creator**: Saturn, associated with Yahweh/God*
*The **Son aspect**: Jupiter or Zeus, the son of Saturn, known as the Living One*
*And the **Holy Spirit** aspect: Vulcan, known as the God of Fire*

266

These three Spiritselves were to whom our particular universe had been assigned.

*Of the three brothers Saturn, the Father, matures first and upon His Enlightenment (redemptive repolarization) gives birth (by Himself) to the first two spirits belonging to the **Elderson Collective...Michael and Lucifer** (Elder meaning first born, to be reborn).*

The pre-human Spiritselves of Michael and Lucifer were conceived and born under the sign of Gemini, or the Celestial Twins. And as a result of their birth, there came their sister-wives/counterparts:

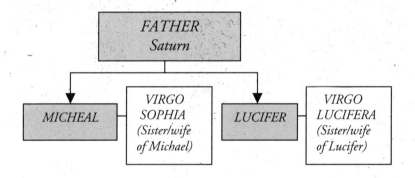

*Michael and Lucifer became the progenitors, Fathers of the **Elderson Collective**, which consisted of two great angelic life-waves (groups). One was the Aries life-wave, which was predominantly male. The other was the Taurus life-wave predominantly female.*

Both fourth kingdom angelic life-waves had their prehuman unfolding (grew up) on the planet Venus. They were known as Prehuman Venus Humanity.

However, it wasn't until the end of the first 5,000-year eternity-time cycle that only two Spiritselves of *all* Prehuman Venus humanity, had finally attained the highest degree of perfection at 100% within their Prehuman Kingdom:

> There was great joy in Heaven for these two Spiritselves, Michael and Lucifer, alone, had reached enlightenment among all others, and thus came to the understanding of the Love Principle...The Wisdom of Love for All Life and All Living...
>
> With this understanding, they were made fully aware of the reason for ensouling – making them responsible for supporting the Trinity in his Divine Plan of purification of the Spiritselves and Creation.
>
> The Spiritself Michael was the first to agree to be ensouled, even knowing that a great sacrifice would be made; for with his ensouling, he would **consciously** loose the wisdom he had attained and the powers that he had obtained as a Spiritself. And with his spiritmind darkened by the physical mind, he would be forced to take on the limitations of the human form.
>
> Though Michael had agreed to this arrangement, Lucifer would not. Lucifer refused to go through evolution again, for he felt it unfair to ask that he should give up the very powers he had worked so long to obtain – and to be forced to start as a babe again...this he decidedly would not do.
>
> Lucifer also knew that once he allowed himself to be attached (or occupy) a Virgin Soul, he could not go back to the Spirit life regions until his Soul matured.
>
> Thus began the War in Heaven: Michael on the side of the Trinity Creator, recruiting those spirits that were to become

ensouled…and Lucifer, intent on stopping the ensouling, recruiting the dissenters, leaving Venus humanity to set himself up in the Plutonian region.

Note: During the War in Heaven, the spiritbodies of the angels were subject to death. And with no Soul to sustain them, their consciousness became extinct.

Meanwhile, the Lord had begun the process of ensouling. The Cosmic Mother's Virgin Soul Nature, lying within the Central Soul Region, (See illus. #1) had now matured. The first microcosmic feminine Soul (#2) lies ready in a Soul-bearing state, *waiting* for a Spiritself to be attached:

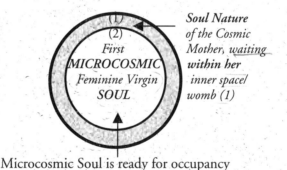

(1)
(2)
First
MICROCOSMIC
Feminine Virgin
SOUL

Soul Nature
of the Cosmic
Mother, waiting
within her
inner space/
womb (1)

Microcosmic Soul is ready for occupancy
by a Spiritself (2)

The Holy Spirit, upon seeing that the first Microcosmic Soul was ready for occupancy, then sent His daughter Ceres/Demeter (the future Earth Goddess) to occupy it.

Once Ceres occupies the Microcosmic Feminine Soul, both are merged as one…and Ceres comes to ensouling (spiritual self-animation) within the first feminine Virgin Soul (2):

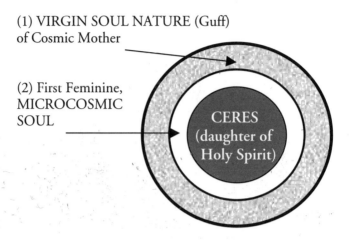

(1) VIRGIN SOUL NATURE (Guff)
of Cosmic Mother

(2) First Feminine,
MICROCOSMIC
SOUL

CERES
(daughter of
Holy Spirit)

The Father, aspect of the Cosmic Trinity Creator, then caused the Spiritself Adam to occupy the womb of Ceres:

Taking the Spiritself Adam, and the Breath of Life, the Father merges him with the dust of the Earth and then fuses him with his Soul-mother Ceres, where Adam experiences the quickening …and thus, he becomes a living Soul:

> And the Lord God formed man of the dust of
> the ground, and breathed into his nostrils the
> breath of life; and man became a living Soul…"
> Genesis 2:7

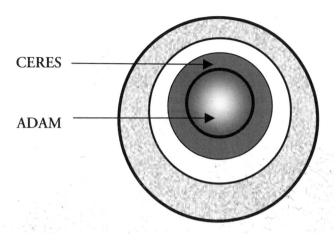

CERES

ADAM

But Ceres, the Soul-Mother of Adam, did not survive the microcosmic Soul-bearing in Eden, for she was not a virgin and could not sustain the pure, feminine essences of the Soul.

Therefore, she is forced to return to the regions from which she had come, leaving her **feminine, Soulbody**, along with its Soul essences, behind...

As Ceres leaves, her **Soulbody** becomes attached to Adam, and he absorbs and assimilates the feminine Soul essences that Ceres leaves behind.

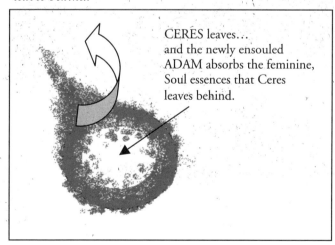

CERES leaves…
and the newly ensouled ADAM absorbs the feminine, Soul essences that Ceres leaves behind.

And because he had absorbed all of the feminine Soul essences, Adam was born as an androgynous Soul – attached to the first microcosmic Soul, as Man.

> So God created man in His own image, in the image of God created He him; male and female created He them.   Genesis 1:9

Adam & Eve

The man, Adam was born in the Garden of Eden, located within the spirit and form regions of a former planet (etheric Earth), whose physical remains are our Moon. The moon, during Adam's time, was live and teaming with life, unlike the *physical* Earth, which was still in preparation for habitation.[*]

Adam loved living in the Garden of Eden. Its peace and tranquility lent itself to the self-reflection necessary for his growth. But the evolution of man meant that there were lessons to learn, and it was only through Life experiences that his purification and understanding would come:

The Lord sent Adam all sorts of tests that would help in purifying his Spirit, Soul, mind and physical body. And as Adam matured, the Lord lovingly awaited the day he would make transition from mortal to immortal man.

While Adam's Soul matured, there were many more Spiritselves that were waiting for ensoulment and still had to be provided with their own physical vehicles. But to provide

---

[*] Adam's vital-etheric counterpart along with all the creatures and their counterparts formed the corresponding etheric, Garden of Eden in the central Soul regions.

additional Souls meant that propagation would be required – which made the division of the sexes imperative. This division was not only for the propagation of human forms in which these Spiritselves could incarnate within, but also for the opportunities for Soul growth and the experiences gained through rotating between male and female genders.

> And the Lord God said, "It is not good that the man should be alone; I will make him an help meet for him." Genesis 2:18

However, Adam was born with a *free will*. He had to agree to this division…he had to volunteer. The Lord, knowing this, gave Adam a test that would bring him to an interesting conclusion:

The Lord called forth Adam, and asked that he give names to all the animals and Prehuman forms in Eden – and Adam began studying long and hard, noting the characteristics of each species, to determine their names.

But by the time Adam was through, he had grown terribly unhappy. He realized how different he was from all the other life forms, which each had a mate of their kind.

> And Adam gave names to all cattle, and to the fowl of the air, and to every beast of the field; but for Adam there was not found an help meet for him.

A great sadness filled him, and he cried to his Father in heaven, begging for someone like himself, someone with whom he may share his Love.

With this act of selfless desire, where Love can grow beyond itself, a great understanding pursued – for Adam experienced an emotional repolarization, and fell into a deep sleep.

While Adam slept, the Lord called out into the spirit regions, for a feminine counterpart to enter into Adam and share his Soul…for Adam was to be divided, giving birth to the sexes, whereby propagation could begin.

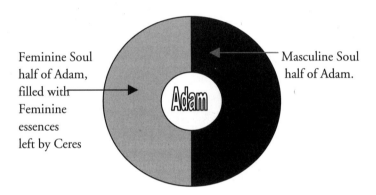

Feminine Soul half of Adam, filled with Feminine essences left by Ceres

Masculine Soul half of Adam.

This time however, the Lord asked for one who was pure, for only a virgin could sustain the very *first* ensouling and the purity of the Virgin Soul. But all the Gods and Goddesses had been actively procreating, and a virgin was nowhere to be found among them.

It was then that the Lord summoned the Spiritself Athene. (As the terms of Roman & Greek myths are being mixed, we are using the following analogy): The history surrounding Athene was that she had been sprung from the forehead of Zeus. However Marie had discovered that Athene's birth from the head of Zeus was the result of his enlightenment. And that upon her birth, Hera had become so angry with Zeus for giving birth without woman or womb that she cursed him with such hatred and such intensity, that

Hera herself gave birth to Satan. (Later, when Lucifer finally agreed to ensouling, it was Satan who took his place).

Though Athene was originally betrothed to Lucifer, she adamantly declared herself to be on Michael's side, of the War in Heaven. And when the Lord called forth a virgin, Athene, though prematurely being sent to ensouling, was the only one that could answer His call.

When Lucifer found out what Athene was about to do, he tried to persuade her otherwise, but it was to no avail. Athene knew that if she did not rescue Adam, ensouling would cease…

This is why Athene is mythologically identified as the "defender of lost causes" in heaven and on earth.

With Athene's support as the emergency Soul partner of Adam, the Lord was able to answer Adam's prayer. And Athene descended into the Eden regions where Adam lay in a deep sleep:

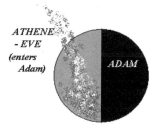

Here, Athene entered into the Soul of Adam, and occupied the half of his Soul that had absorbed all the feminine Soul essences from his mother, Ceres:

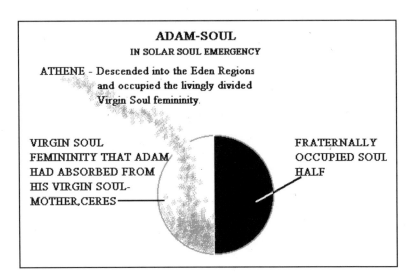

ADAM-SOUL
IN SOLAR SOUL EMERGENCY

ATHENE - Descended into the Eden Regions
and occupied the livingly divided
Virgin Soul femininity.

VIRGIN SOUL
FEMININITY THAT ADAM
HAD ABSORBED FROM
HIS VIRGIN SOUL-
MOTHER, CERES

FRATERNALLY
OCCUPIED SOUL
HALF

Thus, within his spiritual dream, Adam witnesses the ensoulment of Athene as Eve, the Seed of Woman – Adam's Soul is divided as Athene is born – whereby she inherits the first engendered feminine, Virgin Soul:

Soul essences with its added emotional warmth:

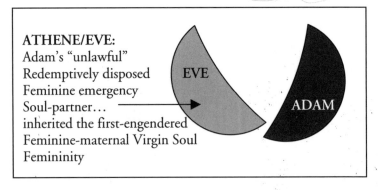

ATHENE/EVE:
Adam's "unlawful"
Redemptively disposed
Feminine emergency
Soul-partner…
inherited the first-engendered
Feminine-maternal Virgin Soul
Femininity

EVE

ADAM

Athene becomes the source of the Eve archetype

Lineal Descent

VENUS (circle)

Elderson Collective:
Michael & Lucifer (along with the rest of the Spiritselves from Venus Humanity)

MOON (circle)

Younger Son Collective:
Central Solar Eden region:
Adam, Eve and Serpent
Virgin Soul Individualization in progress
Former Solar planetary Earth

NEW EARTH (circle)

Younger-Daughter Collective:
Adam/ Eve/Cain/Abel

Cleansing of the Earth

According to Marie, there was a time where the Earth became so overcrowded that "the Earth was divided." It was then, that half the prehuman selfhoods (both natural and spirit) were sent to grow up on the planet Mars, a nursery for future humankind. And although ensouling had continued on Mars, those that were incarnated there would eventually have to return to Earth for further development within the experiences and physical vehicles necessary for *enlightened understanding.*

However, enlightened understanding is sometimes paid with a price, and our Earth had to be cleansed two times to sustain a pure bloodline of Virgin Soul-centered humans. First, there was the *Great Flood* where the cleansing of the planet took place and seed reduction was necessary. The biblical story is detailed in Noah's Ark – where Noah builds an ark that carries his family and two of each animal to safety, while it rained for 40 days and 40 nights. However, Marie believed that there were two arks…a mental and physical one. The mental ark carried creative images of the animals, stored within the mind of Noah to be released after the waters had receded.

Later, there was the *Lesser Flood*, which became the sinking of Old Atlantis. It was said that 64 million human Souls, with all their advanced accomplishments, vanished along with the island of Poseidon.

Then there was the cleansing of the Soul through sacrifice and the Divine Fire:

The First Christ Event occurred on *Macrocosmic Scale* when the Cosmic Mother relinquished Her own Causal Being, or Soul aspect to sustain the Trinity Creator within her womb.

The Second Christ Event occurred on a *Solar Scale* when the Son aspect of the Trinity (while experiencing enlightenment) along with the Father and Holy Spirit, sacrifice and relinquish their position within the selfless Virgin Soul Nature, thus allowing evolution to proceed with ensouling.

The Third Christ Event occurred on a Microcosmic Scale because the human collective had not reached Soul Maturity by their allotted time. Jesus of Nazareth, the Son aspect of God, then came to rescue humanity by perfecting and sacrificing himself for the collective; thereby extending our time here on Earth another 2,500 years. This additional period was called the Virgo Time extension.

Lost Souls

Besides rescuing time, it was also said that Jesus Christ had rescued lost Souls from within the portals of Hell. Lost Souls were the Soul denuded – individuals, who used the Soul *essences,* gained from their life experiences, to reinforce the self or ego, instead of the building of their Souls.

These individuals, having lost their Souls (a putrefied state) would then find themselves in the nether regions, thinking they were dammed forever. But some, within the nether regions, depending on their function within the collective, realized their mistakes. And this realization built up intensity toward the love of the talents they had in life.

This love, built up by their talents, afforded them the opportunity to reenter Fifth Kingdom living. However, this same intensity towards their talents that brought them back to Earth, was generally the very thing that caused them to fall (or lose their Souls) in the first place.

Christ, seeing these lost Souls and the suffering of all Virgin Soul centered humans, voluntarily descended into the portals of Hell and allowed them to reenter the cycle of ensouling here on Earth. This gave them one last chance to clear things up. However, Marie explained, that when we are ready to move on to the sixth kingdom as immortalized beings, these lost Souls risk having to start fifth kingdom living all over again – to develop the much needed Soul essences.

Second Coming

With Christ's *First Coming* he brought the **warmth or Love aspect** to thaw out the cold hearts of reason. However, with the *Second Coming* (which we are experiencing now), there will come the **light aspect**, which will light up our minds to the understanding of God and the worlds of origins and causes – through spiritual insight, science, religion, and other means.

Twenty-five centuries of darkness or nighttime and early dawn periods are behind us and the cycle of the Second Coming has already begun. We are experiencing the daybreak of the Age of Transformation and Enlightenment, an awakening to Conscious Immortality – a conscious understanding of Love for all life and all living – and an *awareness* of our immortality that lies within our Souls.

We are here to develop a state of awareness in which we pierce through the circle of darkness that veils our mortal minds, and enter the depths of our being. There we can awaken faculties within us that have been lying dormant, and for some of us entombed. These faculties are our tools...tools to help us work through the process of purification so that we may be livingly resurrected from within. We are the modern day alchemists, helping to transform not only are being, but the collective as a whole…for the Source cannot return to a state of Oneness if even one of us is left behind.

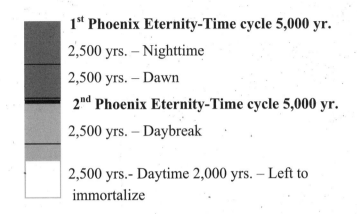

1st Phoenix Eternity-Time cycle 5,000 yr.

2,500 yrs. – Nighttime

2,500 yrs. – Dawn

2nd Phoenix Eternity-Time cycle 5,000 yr.

2,500 yrs. – Daybreak

2,500 yrs.- Daytime 2,000 yrs. – Left to immortalize

Finish

By Desiring from the Heart and Not the Mind...

I am left in awe of the simple-complexity of life...a Causal Principle, woven into the make-up of its creation, to set itself free. A Causal Principle, whose nature is love, and its selfless desire to share this love, becomes the cause of Life itself. A Causal Principle born and reborn expanding and contracting the universe to accommodate its creative urge. This is God as the Love Principle in the Mother, and God as the Creative Principle in the Father – its memories buried within our Souls.

Yet the secret to Life lies before the Big Bang, before man and creation – it is the cosmic web, or womb from which nature and forms of all creation will unfold. Within this geometric, mathematical patterning, lies an androgynous Causal Principle – a selfless, and love-aware intelligence that in giving birth, will sacrifice itself to the sustaining and containing of its creations. It becomes the invisible, selfless, Feminine principle that sustains and contains all Life and all living – for God is *Life* whose nature is Love. It is One – it is whole – and there is nothing greater than itself.

> *If thou art privy to thy country's fate,*
> *Which, happily, foreknowing may avoid, O, speak!*
> *Or if thou hast uphoarded in thy life*
> *Extorted treasure in the womb of earth,*
> *For which, they say, you spirits oft walk in death,*
> *Speak of it: – stay, and speak!*
>
> *Hamlet*

❖

Today Marie is ninety-eight years old. I think of her often and thank her everyday of my life for allowing me to be a part of *her* life's assignment, and helping me discover mine.

DEAR FRIEND...

Years ago, Fred Cole had told me about a small book, that Manly Hall had pulled from his museum vault, the most valued treasure in his collection. An odd shaped book, triangular in form, it was authenticated as having been written by the great mystic, Comte de St. Germain in 1750c. The entire book is written in cipher (symbols), with a handwritten note containing the key for decoding. This book is said to reveal three things: Treasures in the Earth, treasures at sea, and the secret to extending one's life.

The book is now lying within the archives of a prestigious museum, however a copy of this rare text has found its way into my hands through extraordinary circumstances – and yet again, I am faced with another lonely task.

❖

Appendix

THE TEXT OF NATURE

THE TEXT OF NATURE

I sat spellbound, as Marie described the differences of each of the Three-In-One being of the Trinity Creator. But before going on, she told me of a manuscript she had written stating how the creation of *"written"* form (writing) paralleled the creation of the *forms in nature.*

Her theory revealed that the process or steps in which a *human author* takes its ideas and writes them down as text, is similar to the process that the Trinity Creator, the *Divine Author*, takes his ideas and writes them down in the form of nature, the Divine Text of Nature – nature in the form of the world we see each day of our lives.

As human authors, we use writing as geometrical tracings of our thoughts. These alphabetical symbols combine to rescue our thoughts from their perishability, incarnating as writing, thereby "staying the fleetness of time" (suspending the idea). In the process of our own Soul growth, these written ideas, now have more time to creatively invoke, condition, and purify our human mind faculties, to be experienced as understanding. That's where the "Ahhh," comes from when we read something that resonates true to our Souls.

However, while man uses writing as his vehicle of expression, God (or Life) uses the created forms of nature as its vehicle of expression. And because Life is inseparable from motion, motion too is dependent upon form for its expression. Therefore, motion (i.e., the electronic-atomic arrangement of matter) produces the forms in nature. Here is an example of the comparisons of this creative process:

Appendix

The Tools

A **HUMAN author** can express his ideas by using an active **pen** filled with ink, and passive **paper**. With these tools, he will draw his thoughts, as writing.

A **DIVINE author** expresses its ideas by using as His active pen, the **Mind of Nature,** which is infused with *Life* (ink). And instead of the passive paper, He uses an **etheric** *sheet* to draw upon. These drawing plans will act as a guide to mold His thoughts as nature itself.

Both Divine and Human Authors use conscious energy while conceiving, or thinking of an idea. This conscious energy is set into motion as thought:

Energy and Thought

A **HUMAN author** with an idea, sets the energy into motion (as force), which directs the motion of his arm that holds the pen...

A **DIVINE author** wills its idea, setting energy into motion (as force), which directs the immortal fountain pen (Mind of Nature) infused with Life (ink), into first contact with the passive etheric sheet, (paper).

Creating the Form

The **HUMAN author's** arm unites with the pen and sheet, paper; and with pressure of contact, a release of a small amount of ink leaves a point on the blank sheet to begin the construction of the form. As the Human author moves his arm across the sheet creating a line, the ink-flow creating the form on paper, is always ahead of the created form.

Because the paper is:

    a) A two-dimensional surface (2-dim. Matter, chaos). And;

b) The pen or instrument is a three-dimensional object that can be moved in a three-dimensional motion...

The line the author makes, will be difficult to keep straight and will take on a serpentine appearance, moving up and down in its motion as it moves across the surface.

With expansion (movement across) added to the height and depth direction of the serpentine line, we see the representation or symbol of three-dimensional form. We also see the origin of a symbol of the cross and a first degree of order to chaos.

The **DIVINE author's** first contact of his Mind of Nature (pen) with the etheric sheet (paper) releases Life energy (ink) onto the blank etheric sheet as perpetual motion.

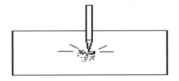

The active ink (five-dimensional Life-energy), fusing with the fourth-dimensional etheric sheet (passive energy), causes a space curdling that begins as a vortex (energy center), which then expands into a first energy whirl. The etheric rhythm, of the passive sheet, has been changed (and with this retarding of perpetual motion, upon the passive sheet) gravity has its inception:

Etheric Sheet and Space Curdling

The motion of this impact flows through the shores of space like a stone thrown in water. A point has now taken form...the first creation, from chaos, or undifferentiated matter has been manifested:

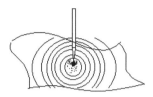

Once the point continues, (as a line) across the etheric sheet, it too takes on a serpentine flow...of electrical matter – electrical matter that has electric and magnetic aspects. It moves in a serpentine fashion, because the etheric perpetual motion has been disturbed in centrifugal waves, and because the electric is light and magnetic is heavier, the flow of this line takes on a serpentine motion moving up, because the electric forces tend to rise, and down because the magnetic forces tend to sink:

Electric

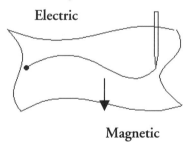

Magnetic

As the magnetic force/matter moves across the etheric sheet it will impart the first degree of order to chaos, causing a division of this homogeneous matter. Matter has now become differentiated as a substance.

In addition, as the pen point (of the Creator) moves across the etheric sheet, releasing the liquid of Life, this fusion has also caused a moving glow of energy as physical light.

And with the addition of physical light, there has now been added another degree of disturbance to the perpetual motion and again a retarding of etheric force constitution...this time, in the formation of a dual substance of electric-magnetic light nature of force.

GLOSSARY

GLOSSARY

As mentioned earlier in the book, it was difficult for Marie to interpret many of her visions of the Arcanum, and she was forced to add new meaning to already existing words. Here is a brief list of the more frequently used words:

Alphabetical thought-tracing: Writing

Awareness: 1. The light and life-*sustaining* factor of intelligence. **2.** The Intelligence of the Soul...Being. **3.** Purely Love-centered intelligence of God; Limitless state; A unifying element; Eternal. Awake; at One; Present; Timeless; Understanding. **4.** Everpresent. **5.** Originally meant together, completely. *(See Consciousness)*

Being: A selfless love aware intelligence – the Causal essence from which all things come forth. Sustains and contains all that is.
being: Sustaining oneself in a state of awareness...God point.. Awake, in the moment. Of and at One with God.
being: (i.e. in human being) a composite living self-individualized entity.

Breath of Life: 1. It is the essence of Life that perpetually imparts existence. Darkly, magnetic radiations of the Cosmic Mother's being. She perpetually breathes in her own being (dark warmth love intelligence), transforms these magnetic radiations, and then exhales it as the Breath of Life itself. Its magnetic love quality is what reinforces the heat that sustains creation. **2.** Sometimes called the "Breath of Intelligent Life." It is the darkly magnetic, space-permeating intelligence or awareness factor of selfless virgin love. It invokes the consciousness (electric light factor) of a living state.

Causal: The first cause. The essence from which all else comes forth.

Causal Being: 1. Essence of Life itself. True nature of God, pure love. The Divine Principle from which all things are first caused. **2.** It is the Fourth and purely feminine aspect of the Cosmic Mother that becomes the first Virgin Soul. **3.** Ignites consciousness.

Coordinated code system: Anagrammatic system of code used by Bacon and his group. Sometimes called *"Invention."*

Consciousness: Is the light factor that *lights up* intelligence. Consciousness is the Intelligence of the Self or Spiritself that occupies the Soul. Therefore, it is "self" centered. Flows through the Spiritmind. It is Limited and self-expending (using up its own life and light) therefore must be sustained by the awareness of the Soul. Chops things up between past and future. Knowing. Transformed and made purified by Love. *(See awareness & chart within book.)*

Cosmic Masculine Trinity Creator: Three-in-one being known within our particular collective as the Father, Son and Holy Spirit. Derived from the three masculine aspects of the Cosmic Mother's being: Self-Being, Intelligent Being, and Space Being (as one). Once enlightened, known as the redeemer creator. While the Cosmic Mother is the causal factor (sacrificing her being as the life essences of creation), the Trinity creates from these essences (in which She has been absorbed).

Essence: Intrinsic properties of or belonging to the core or nature of something.

Evolution: The development of form as it moves through its various stages within the natural kingdoms.

Form Evolution: The development of form, as it moves through stages within the natural kingdoms to ensouling…from the ground up. She called this *form evolution.* (See: Involution)

God: The Essence of Life, whose nature is Love. A Causal Being, sustaining and containing all that there is, by and from within Itself. (See Being.)

God Point: Seeing from God's point of view. A multi-dimensional thinking process that is love focused and based upon a Universal intelligence. On a microcosmic level, it is the sustaining of a state of awareness.

Involution: God dividing Its being into an infinite number of fractions. (See: Evolution)

Natural Mind: Three-dimensional physical mind. It is bound to the physical body (along with its natural memories) and backed by the brain. After death, it will return to the body and mind of the earth from which its form had come.

Original Sin: Karma…which is what we bring into the world with us at birth.

Second heat: Initially, there is a transformational heat, whereby the body and mind is distilled and made purified. Once purified, the body/mind form is subjected to a second heat whereby the lesser form is actually sacrificed at the expense of a higher degree of life.

Selfless: **1.** No "self" or ego. **2.** Limitless (unlimited by the "self").

Soul (Virgin Soul): **1.** Matrix of our being. The Life and light sustaining aspect of God. The only aspect that stays directly connected to the Source. **2.** The eternal feminine essence of all that She is – sacrificed to sustain (give life and light to) creation. **3.** It is a purely "selfless" state, without "self" (or ego) within it. The Soul uses awareness for its intelligence…thereby making it the love aware intelligent aspect of the Cosmic Mother. **4.** Pre Big-Bang it is the Fourth aspect or "Causal Being" (first cause), which later becomes the Cosmic Egg which generates the Souls. **5.** It sustains the "self-centered" Spiritself long enough for it to transform itself into a "self"-less state. This thereby allows the Spiritself to become purified and able to return to the Source. Where the Spiritself is self-centered, the Soul is Love-centered.

Soulbody: Vital-life form of the Soul. Five dimensional patterned body of Life and light. Built from vital or Life essences.

Soulmind: Immortal, vital mind of the Soul. Vital/Life nature. Five dimensional. Occupies the Soulbody. Uses Awareness for its intelligence. Absorbs only the purest of essences, memories that serve as a Divine blueprint, influencing all further development and incarnations of any being or form. Seat of Awareness.

Spirit, Spiritself, plural –selves: Spirit + Self/ego. Uses consciousness for its intelligence. Self-centered, self-expressing, self-expending (uses up its life and light), therefore subject to death unless warmth sustained by the Soul. The "self-centered" Spiritself is sustained by the Soul, long enough for it to become transformed into the "self"-less state of the Soul. This thereby allows the Spiritself to become purified and able to return to the

Source. Where the Spiritself is self-centered, the Soul is Love-centered.

Spiritmind: Mind of the Spirit. Has its own faculties (i.e. spiritual memory, spiritual reason).

Spiritbody, plural -bodies: Fourth-dimensional etheric vehicle of the Spirit. Built of Spirit matter, etheric essences.

Space: The container of the Cosmic Mother's being. Differentiated into three areas: *Inner Space* (womb of God), *Cosmic Space* (Cosmic Mother's home environment) and *Cosmic Space Existence* (where we live and breathe and have our being).

Virgin: Selfless. No spirit or "self"/ego attached.
Virgin Soul: (See Soul)

Virgin Soul Nature: The Soul core or essence of the Cosmic Mother. Gives birth to all Souls (The Guff...that from which all other feminine Virgin Souls come forth.) It is not yet occupied by a Spiritself (ego)...its nature is that of a pure selfless Love. The only aspect that stays directly connected to the Cosmic Mother.

INDEX

Hail Brethren,
And though now I see what has become of me:

I searched the heavens, the dreams of men, and all invention,
To find love's truth in quiet desperation.

I shied from fortune, rich inheritance,
endeavoured art as penitence.

I past through those misfortuned minds,
that thought by education their heart t'would find.

Did meditate amongst philosophically discounted flames,
To find at center, t'was all the same.

Yet hid among some barren shelf,
Its outward show dulled by Spirit's self…

T'was tide, or bond, did draw me there;
While trails of rose and myrrh abandoned air.

I trembled; Soul dimmed my Mortal scent,
So I may grasp its distant waves in wonderment…

Its Answer:
Achieve in One life, within one moment, through one belief,
Yet not for all time, I heard…
Then thought,
at what expense – if any – would this occur?

And though now I see what has become of me…
Hail brethen, it is only Love that determines what shall be.

Victoria Jennings